ORTHO'S All About
Bulbs

Meredith® Books
Des Moines, Iowa

Ortho® Books
An imprint of Meredith® Books

All About Bulbs
Principal Garden Writer: Marty Ross
Editor: Marilyn Rogers
Contributing Technical Editors: August De Hertogh,
    Brent and Becky Heath
Contributing Editors: Veronica Lorson Fowler,
    Leona H. Openshaw
Art Director: Tom Wegner
Copy Chief: Catherine Hamrick
Copy and Production Editor: Terri Fredrickson
Contributing Copy Editors: Martin Miller, Diane Witosky,
    Carol Boker, Todd Keith
Contributing Proofreaders: Kathy Roth Eastman, Mary Pas,
    Gretchen Kaufmann
Contributing Map Illustrator: Jana Fothergill
Contributing Prop/Photo Stylist: Peggy Johnston
Indexer: Don Glassman
Electronic Production Coordinator: Paula Forest
Editorial and Design Assistants: Kathleen Stevens,
    Karen Schirm
Production Director: Douglas M. Johnston
Production Manager: Pam Kvitne
Assistant Prepress Manager: Marjorie J. Schenkelberg

Additional Editorial Contributions from
    Art Rep Services
Director: Chip Nadeau
Designer: lk Design
Illustrator: Dave Brandon

Meredith® Books
Editor in Chief: James D. Blume
Design Director: Matt Strelecki
Managing Editor: Gregory H. Kayko
Executive Ortho Editor: Benjamin W. Allen

Director, Sales & Marketing, Retail: Michael A. Peterson
Director, Sales & Marketing, Special Markets:
    Rita McMullen
Director, Sales & Marketing, Home & Garden Center
    Channel: Ray Wolf
Director, Operations: George A. Susral

Vice President, General Manager: Jamie L. Martin

Meredith Publishing Group
President, Publishing Group: Christopher M. Little
Vice President, Consumer Marketing & Development:
    Hal Oringer

Meredith Corporation
Chairman and Chief Executive Officer: William T. Kerr

Chairman of the Executive Committee: E.T. Meredith III

On the cover: Tulips and marguerites in spring. Photo by
    judywhite.

All of us at Ortho® Books are dedicated to providing you
with the information and ideas you need to enhance your
home and garden. We welcome your comments and
suggestions about this book. Write to us at:
    Meredith Corporation
    Ortho Books
    1716 Locust St.
    Des Moines, IA 50309–3023

If you would like more information on other Ortho
products, call 800-225-2883 or visit us at www.ortho.com

Thanks to
The Netherlands Flower Bulb Information Center, Janet
    Anderson, Michelle George, Lori Gould, Ann Hiemstra,
    Colleen Johnson, Mary Irene Swartz

Photographers
(Photographers credited may retain copyright ©
    to the listed photographs.)
L= Left, R= Right, C= Center, B= Bottom, T= Top
John E. Bryan: p. 11B
Walter Chandoha: p. 29B, 30C,B, 68L
R. Todd Davis: p. 72B, 91T
John Glover: p. 5BL, 12C, 13L, 15T, 16L, 18T, 19T, 20B,
    30 inset, 31T,BR, 37BL, 39BR, 48, 49C, 52T, 53B,
    54CL,BL,CBL, 56T, 60, 66B, 69T, 71TL,TR, 76CL,
    82B, 83T
David Goldberg: p. 12T
Harry Haralambou: p. 12B, 41T, 43C
Pamela J. Harper: p. 35T, 36BR, 66T, 77C, 83C, 90B
Jessie M. Harris: p. 45BL
Lynne Harrison: p. 58B, 62R, 71TLC, BRC, 73BL,
    76TLC,TRC, 80B, 83B
Brent Heath: p. 10T, 13R, 18BL, 25 inset, 37TR, 46BLC,
    49T, 65T, 77B, 81B, 84T, 90T
Jerry Howard/Positive Images: p. 25TR, 31BL, 59BL
Dency Kane: p. 15B, 17, 46BR, 61T
Lynn Karlin: p. 28T
Kit Latham: p. 26T
Andrew Lawson: p. 4T, 5TL, 35B, 37TL,BR, 40T,C, 43T,
    46C,BRC, 50B, 51B, 55, 56B, 57T, 64T, 71BL, 72T,
    73BLC, 76TL, 80T, 82T, 87
Janet Loughrey: p. 36TR
Lee Lockwood/Positive Images: p. 39T
David McDonald/PhotoGarden: p. 14T, 44R, 47B, 53T,
    57B, 62L, 68R, 74L, 86C, 91C,B
Rick & Donna Morus: p. 4B
Netherlands Flower Bulb Information Center: p. 11RC,
    19B, 21, 22, 59T, 65R, 76CRC, 81T, 86B, 89T
Clive Nichols: p. 34, 45TR, 65BL, 77T, Graham
    Strong: 18BR, 30TL; Chenies Manor, Bucks: 26B, 33,
    54TR; Myles Challis: 63T; Nuala Hancock and Mathew
    Bell: 36BL
Jerry Pavia: p. 40B, 50T, 61BR, 63C, 67T, 71BR, 78T, 86T,
    89BR
Joanne Pavia: p. 71BCL
Ben Phillips/Positive Images: p. 46BL
Diane A. Pratt Photo Designs: p. 74TR
Cheryl R. Richter: p. 11T, 46TR, 52BL, 70R
Susan A. Roth: p. 5BR (Louise Mercer design), 14B, 18BC,
    36TL, 38, 39C, 41BR, 42, 44L, 47T, 49B, 51T, 54TL,
    58T, 64B, 67B, 73(BCR,BR), 76(TR,CLC,CR,B), 78B,
    84L, 85B, 88B, 90C
Richard Shiell: p. 6, 7, 8, 9, 11LC, 16TR, 23BL, 32TR,
    41BL, 43B, 44B, 45BR, 52BR, 54BR, 59BR, 61BC, 63B,
    70L, 71TRC, 79, 88T
Pam Spaulding/Positive Images: p. 45TL
Steve Struse: p. 20T
The Studio Central: p. 23T,C,BR, 24, 28B, 32L, 37R, 39BL,
    70BL, 74BR, 84B
Michael S. Thompson: p. 10B, 46L, 69B, 89B
Mark Turner: p. 5TR
Kay Wheeler: p. 73T

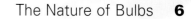

BULBS FOR EVERY GARDENER 4

DESIGNING WITH BULBS 12

BUYING, PLANTING, AND GROWING BULBS 22

DIRECTORY OF BULBS 34

4

BULBS FOR EVERY GARDENER

Concealed in every bulb is a little bit of a beautiful garden. The strange and wonderful shapes of bulbs may not offer many clues to the treasures they hold, but each marvelous package contains the start of a garden of bright colors, dramatic foliage, and great character.

Few plants have the adaptability of bulbs. Through the centuries, they have been stalwart travelers, thriving in conditions far from their native lands.

Tulips are the world's favorite bulb and are accomplished globetrotters. Originally from Asia and the Mediterranean but propagated most famously in Holland, they are exported all over the world by the billions. Also loved worldwide, cannas and caladiums, too, flourish in gardens thousands of miles from their tropical homes. Bulbs from the Amazon are perfectly happy blooming on California decks, and those from China and Japan have colonized many a garden in the Midwest.

These flowers enliven our gardens through every season. As the spectacular bulbs of spring—tulips, daffodils, hyacinths, crocuses, and many others—begin to fade, irises and ornamental onions begin their show. Then tuberous begonias, dahlias, gladioluses, and elephant's ears bring their exuberance to summer gardens. Lilies of all kinds bloom throughout summer, followed by surprise lilies and autumn crocus in the fall. For gardeners in cold climates, winter is the season of beautiful forced bulbs indoors, of fragrant paperwhite daffodils and flashy amaryllis.

Some of the showiest and least demanding houseplants grow from bulbs. A pot of cyclamens will bloom for months indoors; luxurious clivias produce masses of blossoms throughout late winter and early spring. Dwarf cannas, small dahlias, and tuberous begonias also can be successfully grown on bright windowsills.

Throughout the year, the international bulb industry also provides us with a staggering selection of beautiful cut flowers for cheerful bouquets and grand flower arrangements.

This season-defying feat is possible because the industry takes advantage of the bloom seasons of bulbs throughout the whole world. Even in the dead of winter, you can find fresh and lovely lilies, anemones, calla lilies, and gladioluses in neighborhood flower shops.

Bulbs are extremely easy to grow. They are naturally adapted to challenging conditions. Many bulbs can take perfectly good care of themselves, but they will flourish best if you learn about their horticultural needs and their cycles of growth and dormancy.

And best of all, they will thrill you with generous blooms the first year. Most will grow and multiply impressively as the years go by. They will proudly uphold the order and discipline of a formal garden design, and will adapt effortlessly to the tumble of flowers in the most relaxed of garden settings.

Wherever you live and whatever the style or size of your garden, you can grow bulbs. Plant them with confidence: They will not disappoint you.

Delicate snowdrops (above) are often the first flower of the year, coming up through the snow. Lily-flowered tulips (right) have a formal bearing, whether in the garden or in a vase.

A path of irregular fieldstones leads the way through a cottage garden where bright red and yellow tulips bloom among the emerging perennials in dappled sun.

This exuberant summer garden includes many bulbs. Stunning white 'Casa Blanca' lilies bloom with 'Stella d'Oro' daylilies and bright red 'Lucifer' montbretia.

An established planting of fall-blooming autumn crocus may send up dozens of flowers for several weeks in early fall. Other fall-blooming species bloom even later in the season.

Amaryllis are among the most dramatic bulbs for pots indoors. A large bulb may produce one or two flower stalks in late winter or early spring, each with four flaring trumpet-shaped flowers.

THE NATURE OF BULBS

Gardeners use the word "bulb" to refer to any plant that stores energy for its seasonal cycle in an underground storage organ.

Actually, only some of these plants are truly bulbs. What gardeners casually call bulbs can more technically be divided into five categories: true bulbs, corms, tubers, rhizomes, and tuberous roots. No matter what kind of storage organ the plant has, all serve the same general function. They store food to carry the plants through dormancy and to get them started the following growing season.

True dormancy does not exist in bulbs. Although little or no external growth is visible, the bulb continues to develop. In tulips, for example, flower buds form during dormancy. In nature, dormancy is usually brought on by either winter's cold or summer's dryness. In some climates, far from a bulb's native environment, gardeners may induce dormancy by withholding water or digging up and storing the bulb. For example, tender bulbs, such as dahlias or cannas, cannot tolerate frozen soil. But by digging them up and drying them, they will go dormant. You can then store them in a frost-free place all winter long.

Every bulb is a wonderful package. A tulip bulb dug up in the spring shows the parent bulb, roots, foliage, and flower.

A true bulb is a tidy package of fleshy scales with a small basal plate and a shoot that emerges from deep within the bulb.

Scales are modified leaves and contain the food necessary to sustain the bulb during dormancy and early growth. They may be loose and open like those of a lily, or tight and compact like those of a hyacinth.

If a tight bulb is cut in half horizontally, the scales are visible as rings.

During the growing season, new bulbs (called bulblets or offsets) form from buds next to or around the edges of the scales at the bottom of the bulb.

Tulips, daffodils, hyacinths, amaryllis, ornamental onion, snowdrops, and lilies are all true bulbs.

True bulbs come in all sizes and shapes. Clockwise from top right: Purple hyacinth bulbs hint at the color of the flower to come; three scilla bulbs; a large amaryllis bulb with its fleshy roots; surprise lily, already sprouting; a summer-blooming spider lily bulb; five tiny snowdrop bulbs; and two narcissus, one with two "daughter" bulbs.

A variety of corms for all seasons, each with a netted tunic. The five on the right are spring-flowering crocuses; at bottom left are three gladiolus corms, seen from the top where foliage and flower stem emerge; at top left, three freesia corms.

CORMS

A corm is a stem that is modified into a mass of storage tissue. Foliage and flowers arise from buds on the stem. Corms usually are round and slightly flattened, not pointed like a true bulb. If you cut one in half, you won't see scale rings.

The tunics of corms tend to be netted or fibrous. At the top are one or more growing points, or eyes; at the bottom, roots grow from a basal plate. As the plant grows, the old corm shrivels, and new corms—called cormels—form around it. If a new cormel is large, it may produce flowers the following year, but normally it takes two to three years.

Crocuses, montbretia, and gladioluses are typical corms. Autumn crocus, freesias, and dog's tooth violets also are corms.

INSIDE A TRUE BULB

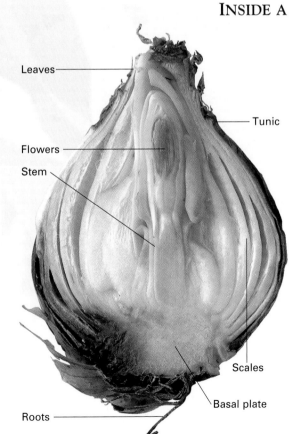

Leaves—
Tunic
Flowers—
Stem—
Scales
Basal plate
Roots—

Slice through a tulip, daffodil, hyacinth, or amaryllis bulb at planting time and you will see a complete embryonic plant inside, with tiny flowers, stems, leaves, and roots. The scales, which surround the embryo, store food for the plant. In many bulbs, a paper-thin tunic protects the scales (lilies do not have a tunic). The roots emerge from the bulb's basal plate, which also holds the scales together.

Some bulbs reproduce by a process called annual replacement. In tulips and ornamental onions, the old bulb, called the "mother" bulb, dies after flowering and is replaced by new "daughter" bulbs of varying sizes. When conditions are right, the largest of these will flower the following season, and the others will bloom in subsequent years.

Other bulbs, such as daffodils and hyacinths, reproduce by offsets. In these bulbs, the "mother" bulb continues to grow for two to three years, and the new bulbs, called offsets, are produced alongside the "mother" bulb. Offsets can be removed and planted elsewhere in the garden.

A true bulb is a complete package with next year's flower already forming inside.

THE NATURE OF BULBS
continued

Tubers may be shriveled and hard or slightly fleshy. At the top are five small winter-aconite tubers; in the center are two gloriosa lilies; on the bottom are three greek anemone tubers (left) and a caladium tuber on the right.

The two rhizomes on the left are canna lilies. The rhizome on the right is an iris, already showing some foliage.

TUBERS

Like a corm, a tuber is a solid mass of food-storing stem, but it lacks both a basal plate and tuniclike covering. Roots and shoots grow from growth buds, which are called eyes, on the surface of the tuber. Some tubers, such as caladiums, diminish in size as the plants grow, and new tubers form at the eyes. Others, such as tuberous begonias, increase in size as they store nutrients during the growing season and develop new growth buds at the same time.

Tubers come in different shapes. Those of tuberous begonias and cyclamen are round and rather flat. Poppy anemone and Greek anemone tubers are odd-shaped and rough-textured. Gloxinias, caladiums, gloriosa lilies—and potatoes—also grow from tubers.

RHIZOMES

Rhizomes are thickened, branching storage stems. They are solid, like corms and tubers, but do not have tunics.

Most rhizomes grow laterally just along or slightly below the surface of the soil, but some rhizomes grow several inches deep. Roots develop on the underside of the rhizome, and during the growing season new plants sprout from buds along the top. To propagate rhizomes, cut the parent into sections, making sure each one contains an eye.

Cannas, calla lilies, corydalises, and lilies-of-the-valley are all rhizomes. Some types of iris grow from rhizomes; others are true bulbs. Still others form fibrous roots like those of most perennials. Wood anemone is a rhizome, but its relatives, Greek anemone and poppy anemone, are tubers.

THE LIFE CYCLE OF A BULB

A daffodil bulb with roots emerging.

The shoot starts to grow.

All bulbous plants have the ability to store food to carry them over a dormant period—whether it is a long winter or a dry summer—until the plant can once again sustain leaves and flowers. When you plant a daffodil bulb in fall, it is dormant, but the flowers for the following spring have already formed within. As the soil temperature drops and rain falls, the bulb begins to root.

TUBEROUS ROOTS

Tuberous roots look like tubers but are actually swollen nutrient-storing root tissue. During the growing season, they put out fibrous roots to take up moisture and nutrients. New growth buds, or eyes, appear at the base of the stem where it joins the tuberous root. This area is called the crown. To divide, cut off a section of the tuberous root with a portion of the crown containing an eye. Daylilies, dahlias, and foxtail lilies grow from tuberous roots.

The tuberous roots of dahlias (bottom left) resemble a cluster of sausages. The three small tuberous roots of persian buttercup (top left) are on their sides. Summer-blooming hardy gloxinias (right) look like a bunch of pale carrots.

The foliage continues to push up, and roots spread into the soil.

Leaves and flowers fully open, and daughter bulbs start to develop.

The foliage fades and the bulb's dormant season begins.

During the coldest part of winter, the shoots usually remain at or just below the surface of the soil and roots may stop growing.

When days lengthen in spring and the soil warms up, the foliage begins to poke through the soil surface and the roots extend their reach. The leaves grow vigorously with the spring rains.

Underground the bulb begins to reproduce.

If you were to dig up a daffodil in March or April, you would see offsets developing at the base of the bulb. These buds become the daffodil's "daughter" bulbs, and they continue to grow while the flowers bloom.

Even as the flowers bloom and fade, the plant's leaves and roots are

producing and storing food inside the bulb. Next year's flowers are developing. The leaves may stay green in the garden for two to three months, and during this period the plant needs moisture.

When the foliage withers, the main bulb and the new small bulbs around its base again enter their dormant period.

Holland's bulb fields are awash with color in spring; red and orange tulips, at the height of their bloom, dominate this landscape. Tulips come from the Mediterranean, but they are propagated by the billions in Holland.

BULB ORIGINS

Most bulbs share a common solution to an environmental problem. They take advantage of a relatively brief period of good weather to store energy (in the form of starch or carbohydrate) and remain dormant during unfavorable—to them—conditions. When the weather is suitable, they use the stored energy to grow and flower.

MEDITERRANEAN CLIMATES

Most bulbs—including many familiar spring-flowering bulbs—come from areas with Mediterranean climates where summers are extremely dry. In this climate, bulbs store nourishment after blooming in the rainy winter and spring, then go dormant for the long, dry summer. These bulbs are so perfectly adapted to harsh summers that they rot if exposed to too much moisture during the hot season. However, if planted in soil that drains well, most cultivated bulbs of Mediterranean origin tolerate summer rain. The sandy soil of Holland has proved an ideal environment.

The Mediterranean climate prevails from southern Europe and northwest Africa to Asia Minor and well into the interior of Asia. Most

These purple spikes of North American-native camass bloom in the spring at the Columbia River Gorge National Scenic Area.

WHERE WINTERS ARE COLD

Some bulbs originate in temperate climates where winters are cold. Tulips and daffodils, for example, come from mountainous regions. Except for parts of the West and Southeast, the United States generally has cold, snowy winters and warm, fairly rainy summers. Lilies, jack-in-the-pulpit, dog's tooth violet, and wake robins are native in this environment throughout the northern hemisphere.

CENTURIES OF TULIPS

Gardeners tend to associate tulips with the bulb fields of Holland, but tulips are actually native to the Mediterranean region—Greece, Turkey, Syria, and Morocco—and are thought to have been imported to Holland from Turkey in the sixteenth century.

In 1593, the great botanist Charles d'Ecluse (better known by the Latin form of his name, Carolus Clusius) left his job as the imperial gardener in Vienna and moved to Holland. There he took a position as professor of botany at Leiden University, which is in an area that has come to be known as Holland's bulb district. In the autumn of 1594, he planted tulips at the university's botanical garden. These were the first tulips ever planted in the sandy Dutch soil. Now an enormous Holland bulb industry produces 3 billion tulips a year.

In the late sixteenth and early seventeenth centuries, tulips were so rare and so costly that only the very rich could afford them. "Tulipomania" swept through the upper levels of society, and tulip fanciers paid extravagant sums for bulbs. The most valuable tulips had "broken" flowers with flames of color swirling through the petals.

According to an invoice of the time, a single tulip bulb was sold for two cartloads of wheat, four cartloads of rye, four fat oxen, five pigs, four tubs of ale, two hogsheads of wine, and 1,000 pounds of cheese. A great speculative market arose followed by a devastating crash in 1637.

Now popular tulip varieties sell for about 50 cents each—but even this small investment returns princely rewards in the spring garden.

species of narcissus, crocus, hyacinth, and grape hyacinth, and some other spring-blooming bulbs, have their origins there. Similar climates are found in California, Chile, Australia, and the southwestern part of South Africa.

SOUTH AFRICAN CLIMATES

Part of South Africa has Mediterranean-like wet winters and dry summers where native bulbs, such as African corn lily, freesia, and baboon flower, bloom in winter or spring. These bulbs must be planted where they will receive only minimal watering during summer. However, much of the rest of the country has the opposite climate: mild, bright, dry winters and wet summers. Bulbs from these areas, including montbretia, guernsey lily, and pineapple lily, need to be dug up and stored for the winter in most parts of North America.

TROPICAL CLIMATES

In the equatorial tropics, rain falls in every season, though often with enough variation that native bulbs have periods of active growth and periods of relative dormancy. Bulbs from the wet tropics are typically evergreen or semideciduous, and in cultivation must never dry out completely. Many bulbs commonly grown as houseplants are from these tropical regions, including clivias, calla lilies, caladiums, orchid pansies, cannas, and gingers.

Tulips and many other bulbs are well adapted to the cool, rainy springs of North America. Good drainage helps them survive wet summers, when they are dormant and don't need water.

Milk-and-wine lilies form enormous clumps in their native tropical home. They thrive where temperatures rarely fall below freezing. In areas with cold winters, grow them in pots.

This field on the Turkish coast near Izmir is typical of the native habitat for anemones. Mediterranean bulbs bloom during rainy winters and springs and are dormant during dry summer months.

BILLIONS OF BULBS

A 17th-century watercolor of tulips

Holland is the world's largest producer of flower bulbs. About 9 billion bulbs are grown every year on a little more than 44,000 acres, and 7 billion of those bulbs are exported around the world.

The production figures reveal a lot about consumer tastes. The United States, for example, imports more than 1 billion Dutch bulbs every year—more than any other country. Americans spend about $500 million a year on bulbs.

Japan is the second-largest importer of Dutch bulbs and Canada the eighth. Most of the bulbs bought by Americans and Canadians are planted by gardeners, but about one-third are bought by the commercial bulb forcing industry to supply florists.

Tulips are the most popular and most widely recognized bulb. There are thousands of cultivars on the market, including top-selling 'Parade' (red), 'Oxford' (yellow), 'Angelique' (blush pink), 'Apricot Beauty' (salmon), and 'Pink Impression' (rose). These are sturdy, showy tulips, and all, except 'Apricot Beauty', can be relied upon to bloom for several years. Although 'Apricot Beauty' is not a great perennializer, it is one of the best tulips for forcing into bloom indoors in winter.

After tulips, two summer bulbs—gladioluses and lilies—are the most popular in the United States, followed by irises, crocuses, daffodils, anemones, and hyacinths.

Pretty clusters of the daffodil 'Hawera' bloom in a cloud of blue forget-me-nots along a path in an informal garden.

Thousands of tall rosy Triumph tulips rise from a sea of yellow pansies in a formal display garden. The pansies are planted after the tulip bulbs in the fall. Across the path, the daffodil 'Tuesday's Child' is in full bloom.

Purple and white crocuses have spread to form a brilliant blanket of bloom around a tree trunk. The crocus foliage must not be mowed until it has begun to turn yellow.

DESIGNING WITH BULBS

Daffodil and hyacinth bulbs can be crowded into pots for a splash of spring color on the stairs. These daffodils are 'Tete-a-Tete'.

Tulips of every description can be combined in a lush and exuberant bouquet that leaves no doubt about the season.

Bulbs are endlessly adaptable in garden design, whether you use them indoors or out, in gardens large or small, or formal or informal.

Drifts of naturalized daffodils and snowdrops, for example, can turn a springtime lawn into a grassy garden meadow. Flashy begonias planted in pretty pots can waltz their way down porch steps, offering a cheerful welcome to visitors. And in a formal, symmetrical garden, stately white tulips can be underplanted with blue pansies and bordered by low hedges of boxwood.

Bulbs can be used in many other ways. On late summer evenings, the perfume from a clump of tuberoses will waft you a long way toward paradise. Dahlias of all colors and sizes can run riot among the perennials of a summer border or fill a window box or patio planter with brilliant color and lush foliage. And a pot of cyclamen from the supermarket will bloom indoors for months, asking very little in return.

Designing with bulbs is no different from laying out other plantings. Your bulb plantings should be a natural expression of your tastes and interests and should reflect the nature of your garden setting.

The style of your house, the way it sits in the landscape, and the placement of buildings, paths, fences, and trees will both inspire and constrain your design.

It is a maxim of garden design that the plants come last, filling out and embellishing the garden plan. When you're ready to think about plants, bulbs are a smart starting point. Good bulb plantings can be the foundation of a lively and attractive garden.

Bulbs provide a tremendous burst of spring color. Few flowers stop traffic as reliably as a mass planting of tulips along the front walk. In summer, too, flashing wands of gladiolus or the bright and fragrant blossoms of tropical gingers add a showy flourish.

Many bulbs ease the transition from one season to the next. Crocus blooms while it is still winter. Ornamental onions are at their height when roses start to bloom. At the end of summer, when annuals begin to fade, spider lilies and autumn crocuses extend the gardening season well into fall.

Some bulbs make an unforgettable but temporary show in the garden: Tulips poke through the soil, bloom, and fade within two months. Others develop more slowly and last longer—canna lilies unfurl countless beautiful and exotic leaves over the course of a summer before they produce their vivid flowers.

Bulbs are so useful and so versatile as to be practically indispensable. It is hard to imagine a good garden design that does not incorporate them in a variety of ways. Garden design is divided into two styles: formal and informal. Bulbs have a place in both.

Just about any plant combination works in an informal garden. Here, blue wood hyacinths bloom among wake robins. After the bulbs fade, hellebores, epimediums, and other woodland perennials take over.

INFORMAL GARDENS

Lush, natural exuberance of flowers and foliage is the essence of informal gardens. Plants simply make themselves at home, and the gardener gets all the credit. Informal gardens are characterized not so much by the plants in them as by their placement in the landscape and their composition.

■ Informal beds are curving and natural appearing rather than geometric. Sweeping shapes with soft edges prevail. Flowers and foliage spill onto paths and and onto lawn.
■ The design is built on balance and graceful proportion—not symmetry.
■ Colors mix with abandon.
■ Boundaries sometimes blur. Crocuses in the lawn, for example, create a spring meadow.
■ The combinations of shapes and textures of flowers and foliage may be carefully planned but never look that way.

The variety in bulb shape, size, texture, flower color, and bloom time makes bulbs perfect in informal gardens.

'Carlton' is one of the most popular daffodils in the world. Here it blooms in a woodsy meadow among the soft spring-green foliage of ostrich ferns.

FLOWER BEDS AND BORDERS

The English, masters of the cottage garden, distinguish between borders, which line the sides of a landscape, often next to walls or hedges, and beds, which lie anywhere else. The main factor in successful bed or border gardening is a pleasing succession of flowers. One possible scenario for bulbs in flower beds and borders goes like this:

The garden fills out when early-flowering shrubs, such as forsythia and quince, begin to bloom. Before they are finished, brilliant yellow daffodils trumpet the spring, hyacinths perfume the air, and fritillarias come up to test the weather. Tulips burst on the scene as shrubs and trees begin to leaf out.

The bed is an ever-changing mass of color. Great purple heads of ornamental onions seem to float among the roses, their silvery seed heads standing like delicate statues all summer. Lilies, dahlias, cannas, gingers, and elephant's ear enjoy the summer sun among daylilies, columbines, and daisies. In the fall, surprise lilies, and autumn-blooming crocuses mingle with asters and chrysanthemums.

GARDEN MEADOWS

A sweep of lawn sparkling with bulbs is easy to create. Simply toss a handful of bulbs, such as daffodils, onto the grass and plant each where it falls. Put small bulbs, such as

anemones, crocus, or grape hyacinths along a path or around the edges of the lawn so that you can see them better.

In most home landscapes, a spring meadow gives way to a summer lawn. If you naturalize spring-flowering bulbs, postpone mowing that area until the foliage yellows so the bulbs can store food for next year's flowers.

WOODLAND GARDENS

To create a woodland garden, you don't need a forest. Just two or three deciduous trees are enough to create the conditions in which woodland plants thrive.

Woodland natives, such as wake robins and dog's-tooth violets, are naturally adapted to conditions under trees, but a wide variety of bulbs thrive and even multiply in woodland gardens where the soil is full of humus.

Deciduous trees, before they leaf out, let in the sunshine that spring bulbs need. Then, in summer the tree canopy deflects summer rain and tree roots keep the soil a bit dry. These conditions make woodland gardens suitable for most spring-blooming bulbs and for many summer- and fall-bloomers as well.

Spring bloomers that do well in woodlands include jack-in-the-pulpits, winter aconites, daffodils, glory-of-the-snow, snowdrops, lilies-of-the-valley, crested irises, fritillarias, and grape hyacinths. Summer bulbs for woodlands are early-blooming Asiatic lilies and some ornamental onions, including star-of-Persia and drumstick. For autumn blooms, try autumn crocus and zephyr lily.

The purple globes of giant allium enliven the garden in early summer. Here, these large ornamental onions rise over silvery artemisia foliage and the spiky blooms of lavender. Later in the season, their pale seed heads are highly decorative.

A SUMMER SCENE

Informal summer gardens depend on colors and textures of a variety of plants. Dahlias and lilies are bright spots in this garden, which also includes cosmos, marigolds, coreopsis, daisies, sedums, and blue oat grass.

Bulbs dominate the spring garden, but most gardeners like to combine them with other plants that bloom after spring bulbs have faded.

When you interplant bulbs with other flowers, match their cultural requirements. In a sunny garden, lilies, dahlias, cannas, gladioluses, montbretia, and other summer bulbs bloom happily among annuals such as cleomes, marigolds, nicotianas, and petunias. Or try them with perennials, such as hardy geraniums, coreopsis, mums, peonies, and goldenrods. All do best in full sun and moist, well-drained soil.

In shade, plant corydalis, tuberous begonias, caladiums, and Turk's-cap lilies with epimediums, hellebores, coral bells, astilbes, hostas, and ferns. Where the soil is moist, try calla lilies or elephant's ears with sweet flag and meadowsweet.

To hide fading bulb foliage, try planting spring-flowering bulbs among daylilies, whose emerging leaves will hide yellowing foliage. Use ground covers to hide maturing foliage of small bulbs, such as crocuses. They make a pleasing, low-maintenance carpet under trees or at the edges of flower beds, and bulbs easily grow through them. In sun or light shade, let phlox or lamb's ears do the hiding. In shady areas, try ajuga, pachysandra, vinca, or ivy.

A FORMAL LOOK

A formal garden is one of elegant simplicity, of straight lines, and of well-ordered flower beds. It is often arranged around a central point or along an axis. Here, nature's effusion is carefully controlled and highly disciplined, the opposite of the hurly-burly in an informal garden.

Repetition in the use of materials is a mark of formal gardens. Brick walls, walks, and edges, for example, hold various areas together in a pattern. This continuity can be emphasized with bulbs. For example, you can create a formal look by planting tall lilies on either side of a garden gate, at the junction of two paths, and at the corners of a reflecting pool.

'Golden Apeldoorn' tulips and indigo-blue hyacinths sparkle in front of a garden wall.

In a large garden, rows of trees can define important lines. Underplanting them with carpets of crocuses or with strikingly architectural bulbs, such as ornamental onions, crown imperials, or caladiums, will emphasize the line and add colorful counterpoint.

In Victorian gardens, bold stands of canna lilies burst like geysers from the center of built-up beds, surrounded by concentric rings of dahlias or tuberous begonias. These formal plantings were sometimes placed like bright islands in a sea of clipped green lawn or as punctuation in the landscape—at each corner of a terrace, for example. Elephant's ears, ginger, or African lily could be substituted for cannas as the tall central element in such a design. Montbretia, calla lilies, dwarf gladioluses, or caladiums could be planted in the rings instead of dahlias or tuberous begonias.

Guernsey lilies bloom in fall with clusters of pink flowers on 24-inch stems. They are planted in an orderly row in this garden, against a background of clipped boxwood, dusted by frost. The bulbs are not hardy where winters are severe.

Containers also can create formality. Urns of tulips can flank steps or a walk or tubs of African lily can be placed in the corners of a patio. Containers in a formal context should be elegant, simple, and sturdy.

Hundreds of tulips of a single cultivar, massed within the crisp edges of a rectangular flower bed, draw attention to the geometry of the planting and to the designer's palette.

A QUESTION OF TIMING

Persian buttercups, tulips, daffodils, and hyacinths bloom together.

Many gardeners like to plant beds of several varieties of spring-flowering bulbs so that they'll all bloom together in a brilliant show. Unfortunately, the timing of such a display is not entirely predictable. Catalogs and garden centers label bulbs as "early," "middle," or "late" to help gardeners time their spring bloom, but weather and local conditions tend to conspire against such plans. To hedge, pick midseason bloomers.

It is easiest to combine closely related cultivars (short for <u>culti</u>vated <u>var</u>iety). A mix of various colors of Triumph tulips, for example, should bloom together. You can also usually count on Darwin Hybrid tulips, which bloom about midseason, to overlap with late-season daffodils. Grape hyacinths last for weeks in cool spring conditions and may bloom with both early and late daffodil varieties with species tulips, and with Greek windflower.

Their first year, new bulbs may bloom up to two weeks later than the same varieties that are already established. But, the following year, they should all be on the same schedule.

It is important to take good notes each year on bloom times of your bulbs and those in other local gardens. Of course, every garden and every spring will be different, but the more information and experience you have, the more likely it is that you will be able to plant combinations of bulbs that bloom together.

Note, however, that since tulips bloom best the first year only, it's advisable to replace them each fall. Gardeners who treat tulips this way—as annuals—have almost complete control over the appearance of formal flower beds. The tulips in such a design are usually dug up just as soon as the flowers have faded; in formal gardens, there is no place for fading foliage.

Hyacinths, massed to accentuate their erectness, density, and uniformity, are particularly effective in beds.

Dutch irises, daffodils, and bearded irises also can be used to advantage in spring displays. Plant them in blocks of color, in soldier-straight lines, or in mass plantings of a single variety. Lilies, cannas, and the larger ornamental onions are excellent for formal summer plantings.

To achieve uniformity, excavate and level the bed, position the bulbs in place, and plant them at the proper depth. Then plant other flowers in contrasting or complementary colors. Violas, alyssums, forget-me-nots, pansies, and primulas are popular choices to combine with tulips.

KEUKENHOF: THE ULTIMATE BULB GARDEN

Mass plantings of thousands of bulbs in the grand setting of Keukenhof, in Lisse, Holland.

The 80-acre Keukenhof ("kitchen garden" in Dutch) near Lisse, Holland, is the world's largest and most spectacular display of spring-flowering bulbs. It opened in 1950 on the grounds of a fifteenth-century royal hunting park. Every year during Keukenhof's brief open season in March through May, 900,000 visitors come from all over the world to marvel at the beauty, bounty, and diversity of the plantings.

Keukenhof is a garden of ancient beech trees, enormous rhododendrons, glittering ponds, winding paths, and sweeping lawns. It is a rambling, informal place, but most of the densely planted beds are elaborately formal. Six million tulips, daffodils, hyacinths, crocuses, and every other spring-flowering bulb imaginable are grown to perfection here. Keukenhof makes a lasting impression because it is artfully designed to take advantage of its setting: The meandering paths through mature woods bring the visitor a new perspective at every turn. The pleasure of pure color—whole fields of bulbs in bloom—and the beauty of individual flowers up close can be savored in delicious succession.

LESSONS OF KEUKENHOF: The beauty of Keukenhof teaches gardeners an important lesson: Masses of color have tremendous impact. Plant two colors of tulips in groups of 25—or better yet, 100 or more—and your garden will stop traffic.

Variety and contrast are extremely important. Tulips by themselves are classically beautiful, but they seem even more magnificent with little grape hyacinths playing at their feet.

Generally speaking, it's a good idea to plant low-growing bulbs in front of tall ones, but experiment with height combinations. For example, a dense planting of hyacinths or small daffodils among drifts of taller flowers gives a bed subtle texture.

Keukenhof is open for eight to nine weeks every spring, starting in late March and ending in late May. The opening dates vary slightly. For information on dates, hotels, and transportation, call or write: Keukenhof, P.O. Box 66, 2160 AB Lisse, Holland. Phone: 011-31-252-465555. Fax: 011-31-252-465565. Web site: www.keukenhof.nl

GROWING BULBS IN CONTAINERS

Tuberous begonias bloom all summer long. Cascading varieties are a good choice for hanging baskets. This lush combination of double-flowering red begonias and rich purple lobelias needs little care.

Every gardener has room for bulbs in containers. A parade of terra-cotta pots marching up the stairs brings the garden to the front door. From the street, a window box bursting with bright dwarf dahlias is a welcoming gesture, and from inside the house, the flowers at the window look like a miniature garden.

Containers filled with colorful tulips, Persian buttercups, daffodils, and other flowers can be enjoyed up close, just like bouquets of cut flowers. If your pots are not too heavy, take them to the porch or patio when they are at their best, then move them to a quiet corner of the garden after their blossoms fade.

Pots give gardeners a great deal of freedom and flexibility. You can arrange them to punctuate the boundaries of a patio, mark a cozy corner on a sunny deck, or tempt garden visitors along a path. A big tub brimming with caladiums, tuberous begonias, or gladioluses creates a garden destination.

Mini-daffodils bloom in a window box. In cold areas, force the bulbs indoors, then plant them in the box.

Tall and exotic crown imperials bloom in a pot amidst variegated ornamental grass.

Lilies are elegant companions for annual asters. Let your imagination run wild when planting bulbs in pots.

Pots of hyacinths, daffodils, and irises can be arranged to make a garden on a tabletop. 'Tete-a-Tete' daffodils are only a little taller than the purple hyacinth 'Delft Blue'. In front of the hyacinths are indigo-blue netted iris, yellow danford iris, and showy Syrian iris.

Even in areas where many bulbs can grow year-round in beds, some gardeners prefer planting their prize specimens in containers. Pots keep bulbs safe from gophers and voles (but not from squirrels). Some bulbs—such as African lily and clivias—grow and bloom best when crowded in a container.

When you plant in pots, your garden can be anywhere you want: on a balcony, a rooftop, a fire escape, or a patio.

The great British garden designer Gertrude Jekyll was renowned for her lush perennial borders, but she also liked to plant bulbs in containers. She used them on walls and around pools as focal points in the garden, adding color, texture, fragrance, and variety wherever it was needed. Jekyll especially liked lilies and canna lilies in pots, but a range of luxurious bulbs will flourish in containers.

Bulbs with a long season of bloom, such as dahlias, montbretia, and tuberous begonias, are good choices. Caladiums, elephant's ears, ornamental sweet potato vines, and other bulbs grown for their interesting foliage also work well. Containers of lilies, pineapple lilies, and tuberoses can be moved in and out of the garden spotlight during the summer, as they come into bloom.

The wide paths of the garden of the Sun King, Louis XIV, at Versailles were lined with painted tubs of orange trees every summer. You could achieve something of that effect with African lilies, tall dahlias, or ornamental onions planted in a pair of massive containers at your front door. In an informal garden, you can make endlessly changing arrangements of small pots and planters.

Good garden shops carry a wide selection of terra-cotta, concrete, cedar, and surprisingly handsome plastic pots and planters. Think of them as sculptural elements and look for containers that complement your garden's style. And you don't have to rely on what's at the nursery. Any container will do; even a leaky watering can or an old teakettle with drainage holes in the bottom can be filled with bright blooms. Let your imagination go.

You'll need to water and fertilize bulbs in pots more often than plants in the ground because the container limits access to nutrients and moisture that would otherwise be unlimited in your garden soil.

Most summer bulbs bloom prolifically in containers in the garden. Here, white-flowering African lilies fill a terra-cotta pot in the foreground, next to pots of pineapple lilies and yellow calla lilies.

BULBS AS HOUSEPLANTS

Bring the outdoors in with bulbs in containers. From left, caladiums, wood sorrel, dwarf lilies, calla lilies, tuberous begonias, and more caladiums.

Spring arrives even in winter when forced daffodils bloom. These varieties, 'Tete-a-Tete', 'Minnow', and 'Jumblie', grow to about 6 inches tall.

Caladiums, tuberous begonias, dwarf cannas, orchid pansies, and many other tropical and semitropical summer bulbs make splendid houseplants. Wood sorrel and cyclamens are also showy and easy to grow.

When you choose plants, remember that attractive foliage is as important as beautiful flowers. Most houseplants can be expected to bloom only part of the year.

Every household is different, of course, in its style and indoor gardening conditions, but bulbs are varied enough to give you flexibility. Different bulbs can be grown to suit your preferences by providing either striking, exotic foliage (as with cannas and caladiums), bright spring color (as with tulips, daffodils, and crocuses), delicious fragrance (as with hyacinths and tuberoses), or long-lasting bloom (as with cyclamens, tuberous begonias, and amaryllis).

As to growing conditions, bulbs take just as many varied sites as they fill design roles.

You don't have to make a big commitment to these plants. Spring-flowering bulbs, especially, are meant to stay indoors for one season only. But many bulbs can remain in a pot for years, summering in the backyard or on a balcony and wintering in the house.

When choosing indoor bulbs, keep in mind leaf texture, shape, and size, just as you would in the garden. Large leaves of dwarf canna lilies and caladium, for example, are striking.

Bulbs as houseplants will not look their best if neglected in dark corners, if they're over- or underwatered, or if kept where it's too hot or too cold, or exposed to drafts. Experiment to learn where your bulbs will thrive. Once they have settled in, you will find them pleasant guests.

GROWING BULBS AS HOUSEPLANTS

LIGHT: Most grow best in bright but indirect sunlight. A window on the north or east side of the house may be just right.

WATER: While growing, a bulb needs regular watering. When dormant, only occasional watering is needed. Allow the water to drain into the saucer, empty it, then wait until soil is barely dry before watering again.

FERTILIZER: Bulbs thrive on frequent light feedings. Fertilize at every watering with one-fourth the dosage recommended on the fertilizer package.

SOIL: In most cases, use regular potting soil.

BOUQUETS OF BULBS

Many bulbs produce wonderful, long-lasting cut flowers. Fistfuls of fragrant freesias or narcissus, extravagant bunches of tulips or irises, or a single gloriosa blossom brighten the whole room. For the best, longest lasting arrangements:

■ Select stems with flowers that are just beginning to open, as well as ones with buds that will open in a day or two. Cut them from the garden early or late in the day when plants contain the most water.

■ If flower stems snap easily, pick them, don't cut them. Otherwise, use sharp scissors or a knife, taking care not to cut the foliage. Have a container with you so you can immediately plunge stems into lukewarm water.

■ When you arrange flowers, don't push tender, easily bruised stems—especially hollow stems, such as narcissus—into florist's foam. Poke a hole first with a pencil.

■ Stems of tulips, anemones, star-of-Bethlehem, and a few other bulb flowers continue to grow in water. If you prefer a straight, formal look, remove them carefully and recut the stems every day.

■ To make bouquets last longer, add a floral preservative to the water and recut the stems and change the water every day or two.

■ Bulb flowers can be mixed with other cut flowers or foliage from the florist's shop or from your garden. You might find inspiration in the seventeenth-century Dutch paintings of lavish arrangements of tulips, carnations, hydrangeas, roses, poppies, primroses, and daisies.

■ Keep arrangements in the coolest spot possible out of direct light.

■ Cut flowers the day before you plan to make your arrangements. Put them in a vase full of water in a cool place to allow the stems to absorb plenty of water.

■ Anemones, Persian buttercups, calla lilies, clivias (if you can bear to cut them), dahlias, gladioluses, freesias, liatrises, and lilies all hold up for days in a vase.

■ Remove all foliage below the water level; the leaves decompose quickly and spoil the water. Keep cut flowers out of direct sunlight, and protect them from heat and drafts.

■ Calla lily foliage holds up better if the leaves are submerged in water for a few hours before you add them to an arrangement.

■ Tulips and daffodils look great together in the garden, but avoid combining them in the same arrangement—the daffodils' sap "poisons" tulips. If you wish to combine them, first let each sit in its own container of water for at least an hour. Better yet, let the daffodils sit in water a day before arranging.

Bulb flowers from the garden or from a florist's shop make a lavish bouquet any time of year. Among the flowers in this arrangement are pale calla lilies, purple spikes of liatris, yellow Persian buttercups, white ornamental onions, and fiery red-and-yellow gloriosa lilies.

Buying, Planting, and Growing Bulbs

The spring garden starts to take shape in early fall when spring-flowering bulbs of every description arrive at garden shops. It's hard to buy too many. Mail-order companies offer an even wider selection.

Even beginning gardeners can plant bulbs with confidence: First-year success with bulbs is practically guaranteed. All the nutrients the flower needs are already stored in these sturdy, undemanding plant organs, so it's hard to make a mistake. The biggest challenge is deciding which bulbs to plant.

SELECTING HEALTHY BULBS

Garden centers and mail-order nurseries offer a vast selection of bulbs of every description

and for every season. Always buy from a reliable source, whether shopping locally or ordering from catalogs. It's almost always better to invest in quality bulbs than to seek bargains. With bulbs, you get what you pay for. Also, make sure the bulbs have been propagated in a nursery. Collecting bulbs from the wild can drive them to extinction.

Healthy bulbs are easy to recognize. They feel solid when you pick them up and have no bruises, cuts, soft spots, or sour odor. Some bulbs may lose their tunics, but this won't

WHICH END IS UP?

It is easy to recognize the business end of tulip and daffodil bulbs: The pointed end is up. With other bulbs, it's not so simple. Look for roots, which are on the bottom, and shoots and growth eyes, which are on top.

Grape hyacinths and fritillaries, for example, sometimes have a few roots attached. Snowdrops and crocuses often produce a pale shoot. Persian buttercups are tuberous roots and their clusters of fat little roots should be planted pointing down.

If you look closely—and you may need a magnifying glass—you can see the growth eyes on Greek anemone and poppy anemone bulbs. The eyes will swell slightly if you soak them overnight before planting, but if you're still unsure plant them on their side. The leaves on a tuberous begonia emerge from the rim of the tuber's shallow dish, so plant it with the rim up. Dahlia tubers sit with the tubers level in the soil or inclined slightly down. In this position, it should be possible to make out the base of the old stem on top of the tuber.

If you are still in doubt, plant bulbs in a shallow container and dig them up after a week to look for roots or shoots. On some spring-flowering bulbs, such as winter aconites, it is nearly impossible to tell which side is up, but it doesn't matter. They will find their way.

Persian buttercups   **Greek anemones**   **Tuberous begonias**   **Dahlias**

affect development. In fact, loose tunics allow you to spot problems. Generally, bulbs should be firm, but firmness is relative: A healthy fritillary, lily, or camass bulb is not as hard as a tulip bulb. Each species' bulbs have their own characteristic heft and feel.

Many bulbs are labeled "top size," which means they are the largest commercially available size. These bulbs produce bigger or more flowers than smaller bulbs. Every species has its own top size. A top-size hyacinth bulb, for example, is larger than a top-size tulip.

Most bulbs are measured in centimeters. A top-size hybrid tulip bulb is about 12 centimeters (4¾ inches) around. Less expensive tulip bulbs may have a circumference of 10 centimeters (4 inches).

When you want the most spectacular blooms the first year, buy top-size bulbs. But when you want large numbers of bulbs for naturalizing in a landscape, it's economical to buy smaller sizes. As long as you plant them where they will thrive, smaller bulbs will catch up with their more expensive cousins in a season or two (though this is less true of tulips).

If you order by mail, inspect the bulbs as soon as they arrive. Plant them within a month or two, if possible, because fresh bulbs perform best. If they arrive before you intend to plant them, you can store most bulbs in a dry spot with good air circulation. Some require moist storage, but do not store them in closed bags. Bulbs need to breathe.

Top-size hybrid tulip bulbs (above) can be 5 inches around while those of species tulips may be no larger than the end of your thumb.

Avoid buying bruised, moldy, soft, or damaged bulbs, such as the gladiolus corms at left. Look instead for firm, well-formed bulbs like the one at far left.

TIME TO PLANT

TOOLS FOR PLANTING

You don't need special tools to plant bulbs. Bulb planters—those handheld tools that cut a round core of earth—work fine in loose, perfectly prepared soil. But for most gardeners, they are hard to use. Also, many daffodils and lilies are simply too big to be planted with this tool, so you're better off with a trowel, garden fork, or spade.

TROWEL: Use a trowel for close work when tucking in bulbs among plants or other narrow confines. Measure the length of the blade, and you'll know just how deep you're planting. For most bulbs, the length of the metal part of a good trowel is deep enough.

GARDEN FORK OR SPADE: A garden fork or a narrow spade is a great tool for working with a partner. One person wields the tool, lifting the soil as the other person follows on hands and knees to slide bulbs in, firmly seating them at the bottom of the hole. Then the "digger" drops the soil back on the bulbs.

DIBBLE: This simple tool works well for planting small bulbs, like crocuses, in loose, sandy soil, but not clay: It will only compact clay soil. Poke the dibble in the ground to the bulb's planting depth, then pull it out and set the bulb in the hole. Push the soil back on top of the bulb and firm lightly.

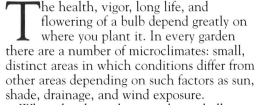

The health, vigor, long life, and flowering of a bulb depend greatly on where you plant it. In every garden there are a number of microclimates: small, distinct areas in which conditions differ from other areas depending on such factors as sun, shade, drainage, and wind exposure.

When deciding where to plant a bulb, select a location with a microclimate close to its natural environment. For example, sunlight reflected from a south-facing wall or fence can create conditions favorable to bulbs naturally adapted to the hot, dry summers of a Mediterranean climate. A bulb native to woodlands will appreciate a site under trees that offers morning light and shelter from hot afternoon sun. Matching microclimates requires familiarity with your garden through the seasons. Conditions can vary dramatically within just a few feet or over a few weeks.

PREPARING THE SOIL

With only a few exceptions—such as Siberian irises, spring snowflakes, and elephant's ears, which tolerate swampy conditions—bulbs must be planted in soil that drains quickly. You can improve drainage by turning the soil to loosen it, adding compost and sand, or planting in raised beds. In many cases a well-placed mini-ditch or two will solve most problems. In extreme cases, it may be necessary to install drainage lines.

Even when drainage is fine, bulbs grow better if you prepare the soil before planting. Break up heavy clay soil with copious amounts of sphagnum peat moss, compost,

PLANTING DEPTHS

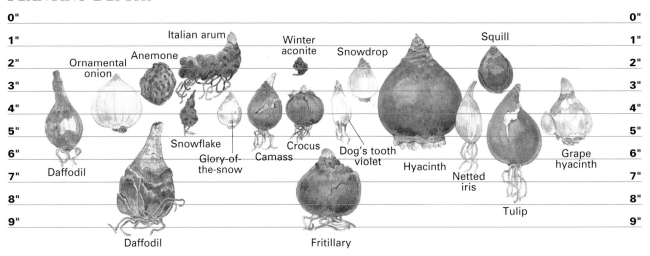

Create patterns of color by marking a grid with string or concrete-reinforcing wire and outlining the pattern with garden lime or flour.

Small bulb planters are fine tools for planting tulips in well-prepared ground, but a trowel digs deeper holes and is a better choice where it's hard to dig.

and sand so air and water can move through easily. In sandy soil, add organic matter, which acts like a sponge, holding moisture and nutrients. Add additional organic material whenever you change over a bed.

PLANTING

Plant bulbs as soon as possible after receiving them so that they don't dry out. Lilies are especially delicate and should go into the ground immediately. In warm climates, keep spring-flowering bulbs in a cool (40° to 54° F) place until the weather cools.

A rule of thumb is to plant bulbs with their base sitting at a depth equal to three times their height and to space them three times their width apart. However, it's safe to say that with few exceptions, bulbs should be planted 5 to 8 inches deep measuring up from their base. Plant bulbs the size of a U.S. quarter or smaller at 5 inches; anything larger at 8 inches. Bulbs do best in loose soil, so if you should plant something 8 inches deep but the soil is loose and rich at 6 inches and compacted and full of clay at 8, settle for 6 inches.

It's okay to plant some bulbs close together (tulips, for example), but if you want them to multiply, leave a space at least two or three times the bulb's width between them. Others need more room. For example, plant giant allium bulbs 12 inches apart. And a labor-saving tip: When planting several bulbs close together, dig one large hole.

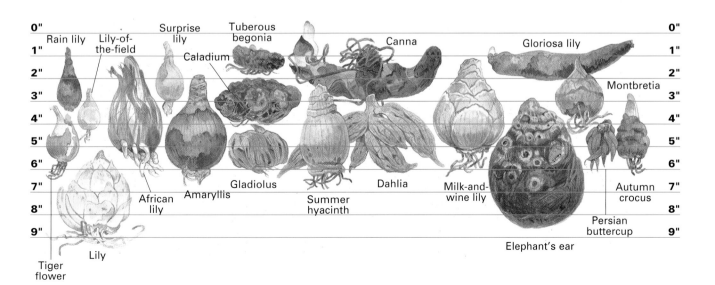

CARING FOR BULBS

After you plant, use a special bulb fertilizer. Follow package directions, then water well.

Bulbs need a lot of moisture in spring. Rain may knock the flowers down, but they'll almost always stand up again when the sun comes out.

If you've ever seen drifts of spring daffodils blooming around an abandoned farmhouse or a stand of canna lilies flourishing for years by a pond, you know that bulbs planted in the right conditions don't need much care. Nevertheless, proper fertilizing, watering, and maintenance will ensure that your bulbs flourish year after year.

FERTILIZING

Bulbs need nutrients to support growth, to root, bloom, and prepare themselves for the year ahead. The major nutrients plants require are nitrogen (N) for chlorophyll production for the leaves and stems, phosphorus (P) for root development, and potassium (K), sometimes called potash, for the general vigor of the plant. In addition, plants need a dozen or so other nutrients in smaller amounts. Soil is the source of most, if not all, of the major and minor nutrients plants need, so a healthy, fertile soil is essential for good plant growth and vigor.

Gardeners use fertilizers to supplement and replenish nutrients in the soil. When you buy fertilizer, the major nutrients are usually indicated on the bag with the letters N, P, and K, followed by a series of numbers, such as 5-10-10. A bag of fertilizer with an NPK analysis of 5-10-10 contains 5 percent nitrogen, 10 percent phosphorus, and 10 percent potassium; the rest is filler.

Although bulbs do not require fertilization immediately after planting, they will benefit from it. Studies with spring-flowering bulbs show that fertilized bulbs perform better than unfertilized ones. Here are tips for making sure bulbs receive the right nutrients in the right amounts.

■ Fertilize spring-flowering bulbs each fall. You can use either a special bulb fertilizer or an all-purpose fertilizer. Follow package directions. Never overfertilize.

■ Spring-flowering bulbs do not benefit from fertilizers applied during or after blooming. High-nitrogen fertilizers applied right after flowering may promote fungal diseases.

■ Work compost into the soil around plantings every year to improve soil structure and provide a broad range of nutrients.

■ Use an all-purpose fertilizer on summer-flowering bulbs when their foliage appears and then once a month until the plants are in full bloom.

■ Some bulbs, such as belladonna lilies and autumn crocus, bloom after foliage has died. Fertilize them while their foliage is green and growing, but not while they are blooming.

WATERING

Water bulbs thoroughly after planting. Except in unusually dry weather, rain normally provides the rest of the moisture needed until the bulbs sprout. However, if you live in a climate with dry periods during the winter, don't let the soil dry out. You may need to water about once a month if the weather is dry and cool (but not freezing).

When plants are a few inches tall, water when needed to keep soil evenly moist while the plants grow and bloom. Bulb roots grow deep, so watering should be thorough. Turn on the sprinkler and give your bulbs 1 inch of water each week. After the foliage of spring-blooming bulbs fades in early summer, they do not need moisture again until fall. In perennial beds and around trees and shrubs, competition from other plants usually keeps bulbs from receiving too much moisture.

MAINTAINING PLANTED AREAS

Mulching with organic material helps bulbs in several important ways. It discourages weeds. It insulates against cold and helps prevent damage from freezing and thawing of the ground. And in summer, particularly in dry climates, it keeps soil temperatures down and retains moisture.

Two of the best mulches are also the least expensive: autumn leaves and compost. Both compost and leaves improve the quality of the soil as they break down.

Before mulching with leaves, it is a good idea to mow over them first or run them through a leaf shredder: Shredded leaves tend to stay put instead of blowing away, and they do not pack down like whole leaves. For compost, if you don't have a compost pile, buy bags of compost from garden shops.

The mulch layer should be 2 to 3 inches deep. If the mulch does break down or if a hard freeze is forecast in early spring, it may be necessary to replenish the mulch.

To keep bulb plants neat, you can remove spent flowers with scissors or a sharp knife, cutting just below the bloom and leaving the stem on the plant. This channels energy into beneficial bulb growth instead of undesirable seed production. Be careful, however, not to cut off too much stem. Lilies, for example, need the leaves on their stems to replenish themselves for next year.

Otherwise, you don't need to fuss much over bulbs to keep your garden neat. Stake lilies if you like them to look soldierly at the back of the garden, but they can lean if you prefer a natural look. Tall dahlias and other very tall bulbs, however, have a tendency to sprawl and usually require staking.

The more bulbs you plant, the more likely you are some day to find yourself slicing through bulbs already in the garden. Labels, photos, or bird's-eye sketches of beds and borders may help you avoid digging where you've already planted.

If you dig up a bulb by mistake, tuck it back into place. Or consider this an opportunity to divide and move the clumps of small bulbs produced by a parent plant. Whichever you do, the bulbs will be fine.

THE PROBLEM WITH FOLIAGE

Gardeners sometimes fold or braid daffodil leaves after flowers have faded. Others like to lay ripening bulb foliage on the ground and mulch over it. All are old practices but ill-advised ones.

Spring-blooming bulbs need their foliage to produce next year's blooms. And the leaves must have access to air and water to do so. So let the plant mature completely through its natural cycle (10 to 12 weeks after flowering) to store nourishment, survive dormancy, and grow the next year. As a rule of thumb, you can remove foliage once it browns completely and pulls away without resistance.

IS BONE MEAL BENEFICIAL?

Bone meal once was an excellent bulb fertilizer. It was made from fresh bone, cartilage, and other animal tissue scraps and was a source of nitrogen, phosphorus, and some essential micronutrients. Today, however, the marrow is steamed out, removing the nitrogen and micronutrients and increasing the phosphorus content. So if you choose to use bone meal, make it a part of a balanced diet that includes another fertilizer containing nitrogen, potassium, and trace elements. Put a bit of bone meal in every planting hole and mix it with the soil at the bottom. Don't sprinkle bone meal on the soil surface—it attracts animals that dig up bulbs.

PLANTING IN CONTAINERS FOR OUTDOORS

Spring- and summer-blooming bulbs look wonderful in window boxes, pots, and other containers outdoors. For them to be successful, good drainage is essential.

A mix of equal parts of garden soil, coarse sand, and organic matter, such as peat moss or compost, makes an excellent growing medium. For large pots, use a commercial soilless mix.

Any container will do, as long as it has drainage holes and is deep enough for the bulbs. The container must be large enough to allow roots to grow and anchor plants.

When growing in pots, you can position bulbs closer together than you would in the ground. Bulbs don't need to be planted as deeply as usual because these plantings are not for the long term. However, you should cover the bulbs with 2 inches of soil. Small pots, and those crowded with plants, demand more attention than large or sparsely planted pots, which hold more soil per plant and thus more moisture and nutrients.

GREAT BULBS FOR CONTAINERS

Some bulbs grow better in containers than others:
- If you live in a region where you can plant spring-flowering bulbs directly in outdoor containers, select early-blooming species and cultivars. 'Stresa', 'Showwinner', and a number of other Kaufmanniana tulips can be planted with early-blooming irises and crocuses.
- In small pots or window boxes, try these summer bulbs: tuberous begonias, caladiums, tuberoses, dwarf dahlias, and low-growing lilies.

SPRING BULBS

Growing spring bulbs in pots is not as easy as in the ground. In zones 7 to 9, you should be able to plant them in containers outdoors at the same time you would plant them in the ground.

In colder areas, pots of bulbs outdoors will freeze solid, then rot. Instead, plant them in temporary containers in a protected but unheated place. In early spring, transplant them into containers outdoors. In warm climates, chill bulbs in the refrigerator before planting them in pots.

A pot of red tuberous begonias thrives in sun or light shade. Planted in the same pot is a tuft of silvery dusty miller and trailing blue lobelia.

SUMMER BULBS

Summer bulbs are usually available in early spring. If you have room indoors for dahlias, cannas, elephant's ears, and tuberous begonias, pot them up about a month before your area's last frost. Wait until the danger of frost is over to put them outside. They'll quickly respond to the warmth and produce shoots. Gladioluses and lilies grow fast and don't need to be started early.

When annual flowers share a container with summer bulbs, plant carefully to avoid damaging bulbs. Keep the pots out of direct sunlight until the bulbs have sprouted. During their growing and blooming period, keep bulbs evenly moist, and fertilize with an all-purpose fertilizer every couple of weeks. Reduce watering when the bulbs begin a rest period, signaled by yellowing leaves.

Fill the container partway with potting soil. There should be room for the roots to grow and spread.

Place bulbs in the pot, spacing them closer than you would plant them in the garden. Cover them with soil.

After planting, water the bulbs. If the soil settles, add more to bring it up to about ¾ inch below the rim.

LIFTING AND STORING

Where winters are cold, summer bulbs must be dug up and stored. Just about the time spring-flowering bulbs arrive at garden shops, you should start thinking about digging up tuberoses, tuberous begonias, gladiolus, canna lilies, elephant's ears, dahlias, and other tender bulbs.

The foliage of tender bulbs fades quickly after the first frost. Be sure to dig up the bulbs before the leaves die back completely so you can find the bulbs. If you have a lot of bulbs to dig, caladiums and tuberoses should come out of the garden first because they are the most sensitive to frost. You can leave dahlias until last since they're the least sensitive.

Here's how to dig and store tender bulbs:
■ Work around all sides of a clump of bulbs with a garden fork, then lift the soil and the bulbs together. Break up the clumps and carefully separate the bulbs with your fingers.
■ Clip off the foliage and remove all soil clinging to the bulbs. Simply brush it off if possible. Avoid hosing it off.
■ Allow the bulbs to dry. Leave them in the shade in the garden for a few days (if frost is not a threat) or spread them out on newspapers in the garage or basement. If bulbs are stored damp, they are apt to rot.
■ Make labels. Most naked bulbs give no clue about the colors of their foliage and flowers. Make a note of the cultivars' names, along with short descriptions (perhaps the height, the flower color, and where you planted them the previous season).
■ Bulb storage requirements vary from cultivar to cultivar, as shown below. Store all,

however, in a container that can breathe, such as a basket, cardboard box, or paper bag. You'll need to use a packing material such as sphagnum peat as well. You may need to cover the bulbs with a length of screen to protect them from mice.
■ Make sure bulbs in storage don't touch one another. Otherwise, if one starts to rot, they all could rot.
■ Don't forget about your bulbs after you store them. Check on them at least once a month during the winter. It may be necessary to move them to another location if the storage area is too warm or too cold. In a warm area, you may see the bulbs sprouting. Also, check for rot and throw away any bulbs that become soft.
■ It may take a season or two to find a good storage place and refine your techniques for storing bulbs over winter. If you lose a few bulbs along the way, don't be discouraged.
■ If your summer bulbs are growing in pots, cut the foliage back just after your area's first frost and move them—pot and all—to a sheltered area, such as a garage or cool basement, for the winter.

Use a garden fork or a spade to dig up summer-blooming bulbs.

Remove the leaves and shake off the soil.

If you need to wash bulbs, let them dry on newspaper before storing them.

Pack summer bulbs in containers that allow air to circulate, such as this bushel basket. Don't store them in a plastic bag. Packing material, such as damp peat or vermiculite, prevents the bulbs from touching and spreading rot.

IDEAL STORAGE CONDITIONS

Different bulbs have different storage requirements. Some bulbs require cool storage (35° to 55° F). Others like it warm (60° to 75° F). Here are some guidelines:

Tuberoses	70°–75° F
Tuberous begonias	35°–41° F in dry peat
Dahlias	35°–45° F in vermiculite
Gladioluses	35°–45° F ventilated
Caladiums, elephant's ears	70°–75° F dry
Canna lilies	41°–50° F in vermiculite or dry peat

FORCING SPRING-FLOWERING BULBS INDOORS

It's easy to bring spring-flowering bulbs into bloom indoors. You can plant several bulbs in one container, like the hyacinths, above, or plant one bulb per pot (inset).

HOW TO FORCE BULBS

1. Fill containers with potting soil so the bulbs sit with tips just at the pot rim. Add soil to barely cover. Water them well.

2. Move the bulbs to a cool, dark place for chilling. These bulbs were stored under a pile of autumn leaves.

3. When the shoots emerge, bring the bulbs indoors and gradually expose them to warmth and light.

With a little planning, you can have spring-flowering bulbs blooming indoors in the depth of winter. Forcing is not difficult, but you may have to improvise a bit, depending on the kinds of bulbs that you plant and on the conditions in your house.

Any 4- to 6-inch deep container with drainage holes is suitable for forcing bulbs. Most gardeners force them in some kind of pot, but you can also grow them on a layer of potting soil in nursery flats, then arrange them in pots or baskets just before they bloom. It's helpful to label the pots with forcing date, cultivar name, color, date of potting, and other information.

Here's how to force most bulbs:

■ Fill containers three-fourths full with moist (not soggy) regular potting soil. Place bulbs on top so their tips are even with the pot rim. Fill in around the bulbs with potting soil, then water thoroughly. It's okay if their noses show a bit. Leave enough room for easy watering.

■ For a lush display, plant bulbs almost shoulder to shoulder. Arrange tulips with their flat side facing the outside of the container. That way the first leaves to emerge will turn outward.

■ Next, chill bulbs for 10 to 16 weeks at temperatures between 35° and 50° F. You can chill the bulbs under a pile of mulch or autumn leaves in the backyard, on a shelf in an unheated garage or shed that doesn't freeze, or even in a spare refrigerator in the basement. You'll need to water the bulbs several times while they chill.

■ After the chilling period and when pale shoots emerge, it's all right to knock the bulbs out of the pot to check on root development. Just replant carefully. As shoots emerge, move pots to a cool, dim area until shoots turn green, then move them to a bright, warm room (65° to 70° F). Flowers will soon appear.

To extend the indoor bloom season, bring in one pot at a time. When flowers start to open, move another pot out of cold storage. Then, when the flowers in the first pot have faded, bring in the second pot. Water lightly every day or two to keep the soil moist because stems flop with overwatering.

■ After the flowers have finished, you can plant the bulbs in the garden if they are hardy in your area. Cut the flowers as they fade and continue watering the plants until you can move the bulbs outdoors. The bulbs may not bloom their first spring in the garden, but they'll probably come back nicely the year after that.

BEST BULBS FOR FORCING

Here are some of the best spring-flowering bulbs for forcing along with the chilling periods they require. Start the process at the beginning of September for January blooms, in late September to early October for February blooms, and in November for March and April blooms.

TULIPS:
'Flair', 'Christmas Marvel', 'Ile de France', 'Pax'—14 weeks
'Apricot Beauty', 'Red Riding Hood', species tulips—16 weeks

DAFFODILS:
'February Gold', 'Tete-a-Tete'—12 weeks
'Jack Snipe', 'Peeping Tom', 'Barrett Browning', 'Thalia'—15 weeks

HYACINTHS:
'Delft Blue', 'Ostara', 'Carnegie', 'Pink Pearl'—11–14 weeks

CROCUS:
'Remembrance', 'Flower Record', 'Pickwick', 'Jeanne d' Arc'—15 weeks

AMARYLLIS

To force amaryllis, buy bulbs when the best selection is available at local stores. You can plant them from October to April. Start them in containers only slightly larger than the bulb and plant the bulb with about one-third of it showing above the soil.

After potting, water the bulb thoroughly, allowing moisture to drain away. Set the pot in a warm spot (65° to 75° F) for about two weeks. Then move it to a bright spot. Keep the potting soil just barely moist until growth begins, then water plants regularly.

Depending on the cultivar and pre-treatment, amaryllis blooms in 4 to 10 weeks after planting.

Amaryllis flowers last for weeks. In summer, move plants outdoors.

Amaryllis should be planted in pots that are only slightly larger than the bulbs.

Its flowers can last for several weeks. When they fade, cut them off and continue watering until foliage has withered. (It will probably last all summer.) Then give the bulb a dry rest period of two to three months. Amaryllis will be happy in the same pot for two or three years.

HYACINTHS

Victorian gardeners liked to bring bright, fragrant hyacinths into bloom indoors in special hyacinth glasses, which are still available today.

To force hyacinths in this way, fill the glass up to its neck with water, then set the bulb in the cup on top. Its base should barely touch the water. Place the bulb glass in a cool (40° to 50° F), dark place for about 13 weeks. Check the water level often, especially at first, until the roots start to grow. When the roots fill the glass and the flower stalk is 2 inches tall, gradually move the hyacinth into bright light in a relatively cool room. This technique works best with prechilled hyacinths, which can be purchased from garden centers and catalogs.

PAPERWHITES

Paperwhite daffodils need no cooling. Plant three or four bulbs in pebbles in a shallow, water-filled bowl and you'll have a show that lasts a good two weeks.

It's easiest to monitor the water level if you use a clear container. Fill the bowl with a 2-inch layer of pebbles, place the bulbs on top, and fill in around them with more pebbles. Add water until it barely touches the bottom of the bulbs. Roots will start to grow almost overnight. Maintain the water level while they grow. When the roots begin to fill the container and the flower stems and foliage are a few inches tall, place the container in a bright room. Some paperwhite cultivars bloom within three weeks after planting; others take twice as long.

You may need to use twigs or stakes (a chopstick works well) to support the stems. Where conditions match those of a cool spring day, paperwhites will last for weeks. But if the temperature is too high (70° is fine; 80° is too warm), or if there isn't enough daylight, the stems will likely flop over. A supplemental grow light about 1 inch above the pots helps keep the stems compact.

If you live where winters are very mild, you can plant the bulbs in the garden after they bloom. Otherwise, toss them on the compost pile and start with fresh paperwhite bulbs the next year.

Keep potted bulbs, such as these 'Thalia' daffodils, away from hot and cold drafts. Water them regularly while they're in bloom. The bulbs can be planted outdoors in spring.

PROPAGATION

The bulbs in your garden are like money well invested: You can expect them to multiply. Some bulbs (winter aconites, blackberry lilies, glory-of-the-snow) self-seed in the garden. Of course, you can also collect the seeds and sow them in flats or in a nursery bed, but they increase naturally without special care.

Some bulbs, such as dahlias, can be propagated by rooting a stem cutting in moist potting soil. You will need to divide other rhizomes, tuberous roots, and cormels. This is a bit more complicated, but if you know the basics, you'll be able to rejuvenate plantings and greatly increase the number of flowers in your garden.

Propagate cannas, irises, and other rhizomes by cutting them into sections.

RHIZOMES

Divide rhizomes of plants such as bearded irises when they finish flowering. Discard any without leaves and cut remaining rhizomes into sections so each sections contains one fan of leaves. Trim leaves and roots to 3 inches long. Replant sections immediately, slightly below the soil surface.

TUBEROUS ROOTS

When you divide tuberous roots, make sure each section has a growth eye.

Before planting in spring, divide tuberous roots such as dahlias into segments with at least one healthy, clearly visible eye or growth bud. Cure the pieces in a warm, dry place for about two days. Then plant them in the garden with the eyes about 2 inches deep.

CORMELS

Remove tiny cormels from the base of corms and plant.

Tiny cormels form around gladioluses and crocuses and will produce new plants. Simply break them off. Crocus cormels can be planted directly in the garden, but where winters are cold, store gladiolus cormels in dry mesh bags at 35° to 41° F. Plant them about 2 inches deep in the spring. A few reach flowering size the first year, but most need a second year.

DIVIDING DAFFODILS

Divide daffodils when the clumps produce lots of leaves and few flowers. Do this in spring after the foliage fades.

When healthy clumps of daffodils fail to bloom, it may be that the bulbs have begun to compete with each other for light and nutrients. It's time to divide them.

Divide daffodils late in spring after the foliage has turned yellow but before it has faded completely. Use a garden fork to dig around the clump, then lift it. There may be as many as 20 bulbs of various sizes if the clump has not been disturbed for several years. Pull the clump apart with your hands. The bulbs should be firm. Throw away any soft ones. Immediately replant the bulbs in well-prepared soil. Put some in the original hole and find a place elsewhere for the rest.

HOW BULBS MULTIPLY

■ Offset bulblets, also called splits, develop on the basal plate of the parent bulb, then break away to form new plants. Hyacinths and daffodils multiply in this way.
■ Bulbils are tiny bulbs that form above ground along a stem. Several lilies, including tiger lilies, produce bulbils.
■ Cormels are offsets produced around the edge of a corm. Some gladioluses can produce up to 50 cormels each.
■ Pips are the crowns of lilies-of-the-valley. They look like stubby, pale fingers along the horizontal roots of the plants, only an inch or so under the surface of the soil. A few pips are enough to start an impressive bed of lilies-of-the-valley.

A HEALTHY GARDEN

Bulbs have few insect or disease pests. Dahlias can be afflicted with powdery mildew and Japanese beetles, borers have a liking for iris rhizomes, aphids may feed on leaves, and some fungi attack bulbs. But because most insects and diseases are only "occasional" pests of bulbs, you'll find the easiest way to avoid them is to maintain a healthy garden. The following tips will help.

■ Start with bulbs from a reputable source. They should be firm and free of mold, cuts, bruises, soft spots, or sour odor.

■ Plant bulbs where they will thrive. Spring- and summer-flowering bulb species need plenty of sun when in bloom. If they have to stretch toward the sun from under the house eaves or beneath evergreens, they're expending energy they could put into growing larger and healthier flowers and bulbs.

■ Do not neglect watering. Spring-flowering bulbs in particular need moisture while they bloom and their foliage matures. Take care of bulbs even after flowers fade. That's when their leaves are manufacturing nutrients to form next year's flowers.

■ Keep weeds under control. A few won't hurt, but weeds are aggressive, and they compete for moisture and nutrients. Pull them by hand after a rain or after you water.

■ Don't overreact to problems. For example, cucumber beetles on dahlias are a nuisance, but before spraying a pesticide, get a handle on the size of the infestation. If only a few insects are on the plants, you can simply pick them off by hand.

■ When you find a problem in your garden, take a few minutes to assess the situation and identify its cause. Without knowing what led to the problem, applying the correct control is a lucky guess. Insecticides don't cure disease, fungicides won't eliminate bugs, and neither will undo the damage from poor growing conditions.

Inspect ailing plants closely, looking for obvious signs of pests. Don't rule out the weather: A rainstorm, heat wave, or light frost may be the cause of a sudden setback. Because so many problems look alike, it's a good idea to take an affected leaf to nursery professionals, who can identify the culprit and recommend a solution.

■ Finally, don't be afraid to be ruthless. Remove plants that are beyond hope.

SQUIRRELS AND RODENTS

Squirrels are great sports that love to find the bulbs you have so carefully hidden in your garden. It is frustrating to see a squirrel scampering along with one of your prize bulbs in its mouth, but there is little you can do since squirrels, voles, mice, and other rodents are difficult to control completely. But you can minimize problems.

■ Plant deep. Even crocus corms should be a good 4 inches deep to thwart squirrels. Water well to settle the soil because bulbs are most vulnerable when the ground is soft, just after planting.

■ Treat bulbs with rodent-repellent sprays.

■ Use protective screening.

■ Not all bulbs attract squirrels. Instead of tulips, plant daffodils, which are poisonous. Other rodent-resistant bulbs include netted irises, Siberian squill, some ornamental onions, lily-of-the-valley, and hyacinths.

You'll find a few bugs in every garden, and everyone loses an occasional plant to disease. But if you buy healthy bulbs, plant them where they'll flourish, and weed and water regularly, most bulb gardens will have few insect and disease problems. Montbretia and dahlias are the stars of this healthy summer garden.

DIRECTORY OF BULBS

This spring garden's exuberant display is based on sweeping plantings of tulips, hyacinths, and daffodils, with pockets of grape hyacinths.

This encyclopedia is designed to answer basic questions and expand your knowledge and appreciation of the great variety of bulbs and the many ways in which you can enjoy them in your home and garden. Most listings are alphabetical, ranging from *Achimenes* to *Zantedeschia*, except for a few special sections. For example, lilies comes before liatris to allow more space for lilies. To the side of each entry you'll find a list of general cultural requirements, including the USDA Hardiness Zones in which each bulb grows best. Use this information as a guideline only. Conditions in each garden vary, and there is little to be lost by experimenting with several different bulbs.

ACHIMENES

Orchid pansy, Mother's tears

- Gesneria family
- Scaly rhizome; deciduous
- Blooms late spring to fall

This genus from Central and South America is related to African violets and gloxinias, but a well-grown hybrid orchid pansy will outshine its cousins with dark, fuzzy leaves hidden by a solid mass of flowers in a 6- to 18-inch mound. Orchid pansy's blossoms are about 3 inches wide, in white, lilac, purple, scarlet, pink, salmon, or yellow. Some flowers are delicately veined.

Orchid pansies are easy to grow, flowering for two months or more. Plants form mounds and sometimes cascade—very attractive in hanging baskets and in large containers.

These plants prefer nighttime temperatures of 60° to 70° F and mid-70° F daytime temperatures. They do not like temperatures below 50° F. At the end of the season, when the flowers fade, reduce watering. Dig up the rhizomes and store them or bring in pots and store them where temperatures range from 50° to 70° F. Leave them unwatered. Divide rhizomes when you repot.

When in bloom an achimenes has countless flowers. It cascades gracefully over the sides of a hanging basket.

USES: As houseplants, in containers
SOIL: Light, organic; commercial African violet mix is ideal
CARE: Water and fertilize weekly during growth and blooming; deer and rodent resistant
LIGHT: Indirect
HARDINESS: Zones 10–11

AGAPANTHUS

African lily, Lily-of-the-Nile

- Lily family
- Rhizome; evergreen or deciduous
- Blooms late spring to early fall

This South African native produces many dense umbels of blossoms on a long stem. Large clumps of glossy, straplike, evergreen leaves are attractive even when the plant is not in bloom. Several widely available cultivars range in height from 1 to 5 feet and in colors from white to dark blue. 'Peter Pan' and 'Queen Anne', blue-flowered cultivars under 2 feet tall, grow vigorously and bloom reliably. Most are evergreen in climates with mild winters.

Larger forms are suited to big pots or tubs. They can be moved to a frost-free place during the winter in cold regions.

Where temperatures do not drop below 20° F, African lilies can be planted permanently in the garden. They thrive even in fairly heavy shade although blooms will be sparse.

African lily is a dramatic cut flower, and flowers last five to seven days in a vase. The seed heads can be dried for arrangements.

USES: In flower beds, containers, as houseplants
SOIL: Well drained
CARE: Tolerates dryness. Thrives with regular water and fertilizer when growing; deer and rodent resistant.
LIGHT: Part shade in hot climates, full sun or part shade elsewhere
HARDINESS: Zones 7–11

Plant the roots 1 inch deep. Space bulbs in the garden 18 to 24 inches apart. In containers, plant a single bulb in a 12-inch pot and three bulbs in a 20-inch pot.

Allow African lilies to become root-bound before dividing. This usually occurs in four or five years. You can grow the bulb in a colder hardiness zone by planting it deeper than usual and mulching well.

African lilies do well in pots where their crowded roots promote abundant flowering.

ALLIUM

Ornamental onions

■ Lily family
■ True bulb; deciduous
■ Blooms in late spring or
early summer

A wide range of alliums—the ornamental cousins of onions, garlic, chives, and shallots—is available today. These ornamental onions are native to various parts of the Northern Hemisphere. They bear spherical clusters of flowers atop straight, leafless stems.

Some ornamental onions are among the best cut flowers, lasting as long as three weeks in a vase. A few are delightfully fragrant. The leaves of several others smell like onions but only when bruised. Ornamental onions remain showy in the garden even after their flowers have faded, and seed heads are excellent in dried arrangements.

Often the last of the spring bulbs to flower, ornamental onions bridge the season between spring and summer. Most thrive in full sun, though a few do well in shade. In the right conditions, they multiply readily. Ornamental onions fit every garden's scale. Some are tiny while others are as tall as a child.

Plant ornamental onion bulbs in fall, 5 inches deep, 8 inches for larger bulbs. Leave them in place so plants can form natural-looking clumps. They will reseed. Divide plants only when containers or garden space become too crowded.

Persian onion (*A. aflatunense*) grows 2 to 3 feet tall with dense, 2- to 3-inch spheres of purple flowers in late spring. It is similar to giant allium but not as large. It is hardy in zones 3 to 7.

Blue globe onion (*A. caeruleum*) is named for its dense, bright sky-blue umbels, which grow about an inch wide. It reaches 1 to 2 feet tall and is hardy in zones 5 to 7.

Nodding onion (*A. cernuum*) has loose clusters of bright pink flowers on stems up to 2 feet tall. A North American native, it is hardy in zones 4 to 8.

Star of Persia (*A. christophii*) blooms with 6- to 10-inch-wide umbels of silvery purple flowers on 1- to 2-foot stems in late spring. They are excellent for dried arrangements. The bulbs do not tolerate much moisture during the summer dormancy. They are hardy in zones 3 to 8.

Small yellow onion (*A. flavum*), hardy in zones 3 to 7, likes full sun and is suited to containers and rock gardens. Yellow bell-shaped flowers appear in early to midsummer.

Giant allium (*A. giganteum*) is well named. It carries its 5- to 6-inch spherical umbels of purple flowers atop stems 3 to 5 feet tall in early

Hybrid 'Globemaster' allium's dense clusters of flowers last for many weeks in the garden.

When ornamental onions bloom, the summer garden begins to fill in around them. Most alliums tolerate light shade, and all thrive in sun.

Sunny-yellow golden garlic is among the smallest of the ornamental onions and is pretty in a woodland garden.

The round globes of stars-of-Persia bloom in the foreground in this early summer garden along with pale pink roses and foxgloves.

USES: In flower beds, meadows, containers, as cut flowers
SOIL: Most well-drained soils
CARE: Water regularly during the growing period; deer and rodent resistant
LIGHT: Sun or light shade, unless otherwise noted
HARDINESS: Zones 4–10, or as noted

Black onion (*A. nigrum*) has 4-inch umbels on stems 2 or 3 feet tall. The white flowers have a dark eye. It is hardy in zones 4 to 7.

Golden garlic (*A. moly*) is suitable for rock gardens, borders, and containers. It bears loose umbels of 1-inch yellow flowers on 10- to 12-inch stems in late spring. Because of its oniony smell, it is seldom suitable for cutting. Plants are hardy in zones 3 to 8.

Tumbleweed onion (*A. schubertii*) puts on a show all by itself. The purple umbels expand to nearly 2 feet across on stems 2 feet high. Individual flowers shoot out from the center like stars in a galaxy. It is striking in the garden all summer long. Plants are hardy in zones 5 to 9, but in zone 5, mulch in winter.

Drumstick allium (*A. sphaerocephalon*) does best in full sun but is useful for naturalizing in lightly shaded woodland gardens and borders. In early summer, it bears oblong clusters of long-lasting reddish-purple flowers on 2- to 3-foot stems. Plants are hardy in zones 5 to 8.

Three-cornered onion (*A. triquetrum*) bears loose umbels of bell-like white flowers striped with green in late spring and early summer. Stems may be a foot tall above ground-hugging foliage. It prefers semishaded places. Where well adapted in zones 3 to 8, it can be invasive.

A. unifolium, native to moist meadows in California, grows to 2 feet, and in mid- to late spring bears bright rose-pink flowers in open umbels. Grow it in any sunny spot, moist or dry. It can become invasive. Plants are hardy in zones 5 to 8.

or midsummer. It is impressive in borders. Plant bulbs 8 inches deep and 12 inches apart. This onion is hardy in zones 3 to 8.

Turkestan onion (*A. karataviense*) produces 2- to 3-inch umbels of lilac or pink flowers on 7- to 8-inch tall stems. Wide, spreading leaves are its most notable feature. It blooms in late spring and is perfect for rock gardens and containers. Plants are hardy in zones 4 to 8.

Clockwise from top right:
Rosy garlic (A. roseum) has delicate, small clusters of soft pink flowers. Drumstick allium takes its name from the shape of its flowers. Turkestan onion's pale, dense globes stand like footlights in the garden. Blue globe onion has clear blue flowers on slender 2-foot tall stems.

Ornamental onion bulbs, like their flowers, may be large or small. Where squirrels and voles are a problem, alliums are a good choice—rodents don't like them.

Peruvian lilies are showy specimens in a summer garden. Where winters are cold, grow them in pots.

ALSTROEMERIA

Peruvian lily, Lily-of-the-Incas, Parrot lily

- Lily family
- Tuberous roots or rhizomes
- Blooms late spring to early or midsummer

Peruvian lilies have bright clusters of 2-inch azalea-like flowers borne atop erect stems that look like those of lilies. Most species grow from 2 to 4 feet tall.

The blooms of Peruvian lily may be etched or blotched with color and are often bicolored. Colors range from tints of warm yellow, orange, gold, apricot, pink, salmon, and red to cool mauve, purple, lavender, cream, and even white.

The plants are fine specimens for growing in containers. Where well adapted, some Peruvian lilies—notably A. *aurantiaca*—naturalize and can become invasive.

Because of its long-stemmed graceful, attractive foliage, brilliant flowers, and long vase life (usually two weeks), Peruvian lily is one of the best flowers for cutting.

USES: In meadows, flower beds, containers, as cut flowers
SOIL: Well drained, acid to neutral
CARE: Water generously; fertilize periodically in spring until flowering ends; attractive to deer and rodents
LIGHT: Partial shade in hot climates, full sun elsewhere
HARDINESS: Zones 6–10

In fall or early spring, plant the tuberous roots at least 6 inches deep and 1 foot apart, spreading out the roots and taking care not to break them. Division often kills the plants.

Most species and hybrids are hardy where temperatures drop to within a few degrees of zero but only if they are planted deep—about 8 inches—and mulched in winter. In colder areas, roots can be dug and stored in damp sand or peat at 35° to 40° F. Often, however, the plants do not survive being dug.

A. *aurantiaca* is bright orange or yellow with contrasting markings. There are several named varieties and hybrids, all quite hardy. This species can be dug in the fall with less risk of dying than the others.

A. *ligtu* and its hybrids have beautifully marked and shaded flowers of white, pink, salmon, and orange.

Belladonna lilies bloom in late summer. Each flower stem bears up to a dozen fragrant blooms.

AMARYLLIS BELLADONNA

Belladonna lily, Naked lady lily

- Amaryllis family
- True bulb; deciduous
- Blooms late summer or fall

The South African belladonna lily is completely unlike its showy tropical American cousin, amaryllis. Belladonna lilies produce strappy foliage in spring, but it dies back in early summer. Then 2- to 3-foot reddish stalks emerge, topped by clusters of 4- to 6-inch pink, rosy red, or white blossoms.

The strongly scented belladonna lily is an excellent cut flower, lasting for about a week. The plants are poisonous if eaten.

Dormant bulbs are available in late spring or early summer. In regions where the temperature doesn't drop below about 10° F, they should be planted about 1 foot apart with their noses about even with the soil. In colder areas, plant them deeper to protect them from the cold.

USES: In meadows, flower beds, containers
SOIL: Any well-drained soil
CARE: Water regularly during the period of active growth; fertilize in late summer; deer and rodent resistant.
LIGHT: Full sun in the hottest spot in the garden
HARDINESS: Zones 6–10

Place belladonna lilies among shrubs or perennials, which will hide the withering leaves in early summer but won't shade the soil above the bulbs. Heat and dryness during the late spring and early summer dormancy period are essential for proper development of the bulb.

Divide clumps of belladonna lilies only when necessary, and then only after the foliage begins to yellow. Belladonna lilies may stop blooming for several years after you move them.

Bulbs in containers should be planted with their tops exposed. Don't water the pots after the foliage dies. Let plants become pot-bound.

A handful of Greek anemone tubers becomes a cheerful carpet of color in spring.

Graceful poppy anemone blooms on a 12-inch stem.

ANEMONE

Greek anemone, Windflower

- Buttercup family
- Tuber; deciduous
- Bloom time is usually spring

Open, fresh, poppylike beauty and lovely colors have established anemones as staples for gardeners and florists alike. The anemone species and hybrids described here are native to the Mediterranean area. They grow best where summers are dry.

After soaking a few hours or overnight, plant the knobby tubers 3 to 4 inches deep and 4 to 6 inches apart. If you're not sure which end is up, lay them on their sides when planting. North of their adapted zones, plant anemones in the spring. Elsewhere, the time to plant is in the fall or spring.

Greek anemone (*Anemone blanda*), sometimes called windflower, is from southeastern Europe and Turkey. It has sky blue, dark blue, white, pink, or rose flowers in spring. The flowers close at night.

This species is also the hardiest of the anemones. In the right situation, it will naturalize where winter temperatures fall to minus 10° F or even colder. Plant Greek anemone in fall in the front of a flower bed or in a lawn.

Poppy anemone (*A. coronaria*) has flowers 2 inches wide or wider, on 5- to 10-inch stems. It is the most common garden and florist anemone. Its showy flowers are white, red, pink, blue, or purple, most with contrasting centers. They last four to seven days when cut.

Poppy anemone hybrids are showier and have larger flowers, to 4 inches wide. The DeCaen strain has single flowers. The St. Brigid strain has semidouble blooms.

Poppy anemones can't tolerate wet summers but are hardy to 10° F.

USES: In meadows, woodlands, flower beds, containers, as cut flowers
SOIL: Very well drained
CARE: Provide moisture during periods of growth and allow to dry during dormancy; attractive to deer and rodents
LIGHT: Light shade or full sun
HARDINESS: Zones 7–10

Windflower bulbs look like misshapen fossils. If you soak them overnight before planting, you'll be able to see the slightly swollen areas where shoots will emerge.

Greek anemone flowers are only about 2 inches across, but they are very showy.

Most arisaemas, such as this A. candidissimum, *are available in pots, not as bulbs.*

ARISAEMA

Jack-in-the-pulpit, Green dragon

- Arum family
- Tuber; deciduous
- Blooms in spring or early summer

Jack-in-the-pulpit (*A. triphyllum*) and green dragon (*A. dracontium*) are native to North America and are well adapted to woodland conditions where temperatures do not drop below minus 20° F. All have glossy, three-lobed leaves that last through the summer. The curious green and purplish brown striped

USES: In woodlands, flower beds, pots
SOIL: Moderate to well drained; slightly acid
CARE: Water generously; deer and rodent resistant
LIGHT: Light to medium shade
HARDINESS: Zones 4–9

flowers (actually a sheath enclosing the sexual parts) reveal its kinship with the calla lily. All produce reddish berries in summer and fall.

Jack-in-the-pulpit and green dragon are often sold by wildflower specialists. Plant tubers about 4 inches deep and 10 to 12 inches apart in fall. Propagate them from offsets in fall or start seeds indoors. Plant seedlings out in spring or fall. Also available as container plants in the spring.

ARUM ITALICUM

Italian arum

- Arum family
- Tuber; deciduous
- Blooms in spring or early summer

USES: In borders, woodland edges, pots
SOIL: Well drained, organic, acid to neutral
CARE: Water through bloom; deer and rodent resistant
LIGHT: Light to full shade
HARDINESS: Zones 5–9

This 12- to 18-inch-tall native of the Mediterranean produces marbled, waxy, arrow-shaped leaves in the fall. The 12-inch leaves often last through late spring, especially in well-established clumps. In late spring, creamy or greenish callalike flowers appear. The flowers, up to 8 inches tall, are sometimes spotted or stained with purple at their bases. They are followed by tight clusters of brilliant scarlet berries, which last through summer. Some varieties have heavily variegated leaves. The foliage and berries are excellent for arrangements, but they are poisonous if eaten.

Plant tubers in the fall, 3 or 4 inches deep and 6 to 12 inches apart. Propagate plants by division in late summer. They take a couple of years to reestablish.

Berries gleam among mottled leaves of arum.

BABIANA

Baboon flower

- Iris family
- Corm; deciduous
- Blooms in late spring and early summer in the garden

Baboon flowers grow on spikes, like gladiolus. Each corm produces several flower stalks, and each stalk bears 10 or more flowers.

Baboon flower is native to South Africa, where baboons eat its corms, giving plants their common name.

The upright 1- to 2-inch flowers appear on dense spikes, rising about 12 inches above fans of short, pleated, rather fuzzy leaves. Predominant flower colors are shades of blue, mauve, and yellow.

Babiana stricta, the best-known species, has fragrant flowers that may last for as long as a month in the garden.

USES: In borders, containers
SOIL: Well drained
CARE: Water regularly through bloom
LIGHT: Sun or very light shade
HARDINESS: Zones 8–10

After the onset of cool autumn weather, plant corms in the garden 5 to 9 inches deep and 2 inches apart. Or you can plant up to 10 or 12 corms into a 6-inch pot, setting them deep in the pot. Divide only when plants become crowded. In areas with wet summers, dig the corms and store them in a warm, ventilated place until autumn.

Where winter temperatures drop below freezing, baboon flower can survive if it is planted in a protected place with a southern exposure and mulch.

BEGONIA TUBERHYBRIDA HYBRIDS

Tuberous begonia

- Begonia family
- Tuber; deciduous
- Blooms early summer to fall

Tuberous hybrid begonias, whose ancestors are native to the Andes, shine in the garden through the warm months. The flowers are voluptuous, with substantial, waxy petals in bright colors. The range of colors excludes only blue, green, and purple. Bicolors are common among the hybrids.

The ruffled blooms may be single or double; some have a contrasting picotee edge. Each bloom stem bears small, single female flowers and large, single or double male flowers, up to 6 inches wide. Some cascading varieties are perfect for hanging baskets, others well suited to pots and flower beds. Tuberous begonias prefer humid, cool-summer climates.

After all danger of frost is past, plant tubers concave side up with their tops slightly above soil level. For earlier blooms, start begonias indoors and move them outside when the weather permits. Use three or four tubers per hanging basket or pot. In beds space them 10 to 18 inches apart. Water regularly, but soak them from the bottom rather than watering from above. Guard against slugs and snails. Gradually reduce watering when leaves start to yellow in fall. Store tubers in a cool (35° to 41° F) place in dry peat or in pots. Propagate plants by shoot or leaf cuttings in the spring.

Another tuberous begonia, *B. grandis*, is hardy in the garden in zones 6 to 8, even when temperatures drop to minus 15° F. This old-time begonia used to be available only as a pass-along plant, from one gardener to another, and is relatively new to the trade. Hardy begonias emerge in late spring and thrive in light shade. They bloom in late summer, and the flowers last until frost.

USES: In containers, borders, as houseplants
SOIL: Well drained, organic, acid to neutral
CARE: Water and fertilize during active growth; attractive to deer and rodents
LIGHT: Light shade
HARDINESS: Most are not hardy.

Tuberous begonias are beloved for their lush, dark green leaves and many clusters of brightly colored flowers. They bloom all summer long.

Viewed from the top, these begonia tubers are beginning to push out tiny pink shoots from the rims of their slightly scooped sides.

Tuberous begonias thrive in containers. Flowers will fall off if you overwater plants. Plants grow best where summers are fairly cool but humid.

The freckled flowers of blackberry lily stand up to 3 feet tall and bloom for weeks in the summer.

BELAMCANDA CHINENSIS

Blackberry lily, Leopard flower

■ Iris family
■ Tuberous root; deciduous
■ Blooms in summer

This undemanding native of China and Japan is valued for its imposing flat fans of foliage and 2-inch-wide, crimson-speckled orange flowers on 2- to 3-foot branching stems.

The blooms last over a long summer season. When the fruit pods split open in the fall, they reveal clusters of shiny black berries, hence the name of the plant. The berries are attractive in dried arrangements.

Even where temperatures drop to minus 10° F, blackberry lilies add texture and color to perennial and mixed borders. They can be grown in containers in any climate. Lift the tuberous roots from the garden, or leave them in containers, to store in a frost-free place (35° to 41° F) for the winter.

USES: In borders, containers
SOIL: Rich, sandy loam
CARE: Water during active growth; deer and rodent resistant
LIGHT: Full sun or light shade
HARDINESS: Zones 5–10

Plant roots in the garden in spring or early fall, 1 inch deep and 6 inches apart. Flowers are more profuse in full sun, but blackberry lily tolerates growing in light shade. Except in areas with mild winters, mulch in winter.

Propagate plants by division or by sowing seeds outdoors in spring or summer, no later than 2 months before the first frost. The seeds sometimes sprout in cracks between bricks or stones in a patio, where the seedlings thrive.

B. chinensis is the most widely available species. *B. flabellata* is similar, but its flowers are pure yellow, and plants prefer some shade and more water. A related plant, *Pardancanda norrisii*, is a cross between blackberry lily and vesper iris (*Pardanthopsis dichotoma*). Its rainbow-colored flowers are solid, speckled, blotched, and sometimes bicolored.

Mariposa lilies bloom best in light shade.

CALOCHORTUS

Mariposa lily, Fairy lantern, Star tulip

■ Lily family
■ True bulb; deciduous
■ Blooms late spring and early summer

About 60 species of calochortus are native to the American West. These bulbs have recently come on the American market, but only about five or six species and cultivars currently are available. They all grow to about 2 feet tall.

Of the many calochortus species, mariposa lilies are the showiest. The three broad, fan-shaped petals of most species curve gracefully back at the edges and are splendidly marked and feathered. The 3- to 4-inch flowers are produced over several weeks.

Plant the bulbs in late fall, 3 to 5 inches deep in the garden or 2 to 4 inches deep in pots, five or six bulbs per 6-inch pot.

Most mariposa lilies need protection from alternate freezing and thawing (mulching the

USES: In containers, dry meadows, as cut flowers
SOIL: Well drained, sandy, not too rich
CARE: Keep soil moist until bulbs bloom, then let plants dry; attractive to deer and rodents
LIGHT: Sun or light shade, depending on the species
HARDINESS: Zones 5–10

bed over winter helps). Snip off flowers as they fade in spring to conserve vigor for next season's blooms.

In areas with rainy summers, lift and store the bulbs in dry packing material. Container-grown mariposa lilies can be allowed to dry out and then can be stored in their containers. Propagate plants from offsets or seeds in the fall.

C. albus (fairy lantern) has white flowers, which are sometimes rose tinted. It prefers light shade. *C. luteus* (yellow mariposa) has rich yellow flowers, speckled and lined with rust toward the center of the flower. *C. venustus* (white mariposa) may have white, yellow, purple, or red petals, usually marked with a dark red blotch toward the center. It is hardy only to zone 6.

CALADIUM HORTULANUM

Fancy-leaved caladium

- Arum family
- Tuber; deciduous
- Grown for showy foliage

Caladiums with their large, extravagantly colored and patterned leaves are at home both in formal and informal gardens and in containers. They beautifully complement impatiens, ferns, and other shade plants.

Caladiums are native to South American rain forests. Where summer nights are seldom cooler than 60° F, they add bold strokes of color to shady garden areas. They also are excellent houseplants. Plant tubers in a succession of pots at two- or three-month intervals, and enjoy caladiums indoors throughout the year.

The 1- to 3-foot-tall plants have bicolored or tricolored leaves in various shades of green, combined with white, red, rose, or pink. In some cultivars, one color fades gently into another. Others have strongly contrasting veins, borders, or spatterings of color.

Plant caladiums in late spring when night temperatures are warm (around 60° F) or start tubers indoors in a warm (70° to 75° F) room. Plant the tubers, knobby side up, 2 inches deep, spacing them 8 to 12 inches apart in the garden. In 8-inch pots, plant one large tuber or two or three small tubers. Break off the first shoot to emerge to encourage multiple leaves and the best show. Garden-planted tubers should be dug and stored in the fall. Some gardeners start the tubers in pots, bury the pots in garden beds, then lift the pots for dry storage at 70° F during dormancy. In the garden, caladiums can be bothered by snails and slugs.

USES: In flower beds, containers, as houseplants
SOIL: Wet to well drained, organic, acid to neutral
CARE: Give ample water and fertilize during growing period; deer and rodent resistant
LIGHT: Light to deep shade
HARDINESS: Zones 10–11

The fabulous shield-shaped leaves of caladiums are variegated, with combinations of pink, red, green, and/or silver.

Even in deep shade, caladium leaves add a bright flash of color. Plant caladiums where their large leaves will be protected from wind.

Plant caladium tubers and plants outdoors after both the air and soil have warmed up. Or start them earlier in pots indoors.

CAMASSIA

Camass, Quamash

- Lily family
- True bulb; deciduous
- Blooms in late spring

Camass are underappreciated North American spring-flowering bulbs. They do not have the dazzle of tulips, daffodils, and hyacinths, but these hardy bulbs put on an excellent show. When tulips are fading, camass flower stalks shoot up from clumps of slender green foliage, bearing as many as 40 loosely clustered starry blossoms, each about 2 inches across. Stalks may be 12 to 36 inches tall, depending on the species, and flowering lasts for several weeks.

Camass are easy to grow, tolerating neglect and a wide range of cultural conditions. They thrive in moist, heavy soils and in partial shade. They sparkle in the dappled light under dogwood or redbud trees in spring, fading gracefully, and colonizing reliably.

Camass also are good choices for planting among shrubs and beside water gardens. They are related to the English bluebell but are native to the marshes and wet meadows of western North America. They are hardy to minus 40° F.

Camass have clusters of starry flowers on tall spikes. Leichtlin camass, here, is a widely available species.

Camass bulbs look like large tulip bulbs, but they do not have a protective tunic, like tulips. They are often slightly pockmarked and may have brown or blue spots. The bulbs are not rock-hard but are firm. Plant them in groups of three to five or more in the fall after temperatures moderate. Set them 8 inches deep and about 6 inches apart. They like moist sites, and they are resistant to rot. If clumps become too thick, divide them in summer when leaves turn yellow.

Cusick camass (*Camassia cusickii*) is from Oregon. The light blue flowers are densely clustered on stalks up to 2 feet tall. The bulbs can be quite large, weighing up to 8 ounces.

Leichtlin quamash (*C. leichtlinii*) bears deep blue-violet to bright blue flowers on stems 2 or 3 feet tall. This camass is sometimes called the great camass. Its native range is from British Columbia to northern California.

Two white forms are available: 'Alba' and 'Semiplena' (semidouble). 'Blue Danube' is a dark blue variety. 'Caerulea' has rich, lilac blooms, which stand out well from a distance.

Common camass (*C. quamash*), from the same area as leichtlin camass, bears deep blue-violet 2-inch flowers on 1- to 2-foot stems. This is the lowest-growing and earliest-flowering camass. The old species name, *esculenta*, means edible. All camass bulbs and plants are actually poisonous, but Native Americans ate the bulbs after boiling or roasting them.

Wild hyacinth (*C. scilloides*) is a southern species. It is native to prairies and grasslands from Georgia to central Texas. It grows in full sun to about 2 feet tall and has a delicate fragrance.

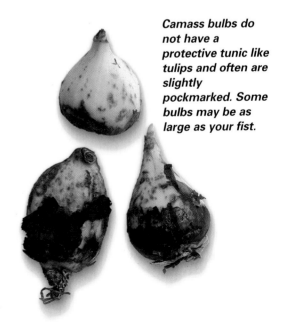

Camass bulbs do not have a protective tunic like tulips and often are slightly pockmarked. Some bulbs may be as large as your fist.

Camass blooms in late spring after perennials have emerged. 'Blue Danube' leichtlin camass has dark blue flowers. There are also white and double-flowered camass.

USES: In meadows, woodlands, borders
SOIL: Most soils, including heavy, wet types
CARE: Water generously during active growth and blooming; attractive to deer and rodents
LIGHT: Sun or light shade
HARDINESS: Zones 4–7

NORTH AMERICAN NATIVE BULBS

Clockwise from top left: From Vancouver Island: 'Pagoda', a hybrid of the dog's tooth violet (Erythonium revolutum). From California: White wake-robin (Trillium chloropetalum 'Album'). Prairie native: blazing star (Liatris spicata). From the Appalachian mountains: meadow lily (Lilium canadense).

Although most gardeners associate bulbs with the sweeping masses of color in the tulip fields of Holland, a number of excellent bulbs are native to North America and thrive in our gardens naturally. In some cases, as with camass, the Dutch propagate these native American bulbs and ship them to customers all over the world.

For gardeners who are interested in growing native bulbs, the selection of species and hybrids developed from those species is increasing.

Native bulbs lend themselves to plantings with a natural, relaxed look. Many are at home in woodland plantings. Others are excellent in bog gardens alongside pools and ponds. Still others can be part of a prairie or meadow planting.

Whether you buy dormant bulbs or plants in containers, make sure that the supplier is selling *only* nursery-propagated stock, not bulbs collected in the wild.

■Among alliums, nodding onion and *Allium unifolium* (see p. 36) are American natives. *A. unifolium* has been in cultivation since 1873.

■Native arisaemas, such as jack-in-the-pulpit (see p. 41), are increasing in popularity. Jack-in-the-pulpit blooms in May and thrives in shade, while green dragon prefers at least some sun and may get to be 4 feet tall.

■Native crown imperials (see p. 57) come from the Pacific Northwest. 'Martha Roderick', a hybrid of (*Fritillaria biflora*), is adaptable in other areas, as is the scarlet fritillaria, (*F. recurva*).

■Several lilies (see p. 70) come from eastern and central North America. The turk's-cap lily (*Lilium superbum*) is a red species. Meadow lily (*L. canadense*) has yellow flowers.

■White wake robin (see p. 82) is perhaps the most popular and the easiest to grow of the American genus of ephemeral woodland bulbs.

Canna, Indian shot

- Canna family
- Rhizome; deciduous
- Blooms late spring to fall

The large green, bronze, or fantastically variegated leaves of canna create a tropical effect as they unfurl in the garden. Massed in beds, in clumps in a border, or in pots on a terrace, they contribute handsome foliage and bold floral color during the warm months.

The exotic-looking flowers, which attract hummingbirds, shoot up through curls of leaves at the tops of plants, like the fancy plume on a cap. Canna flowers may be scarlet, apricot, coral, pink, or yellow-orange, and sometimes they have bright freckles. Heights vary from around 18 inches for dwarf cultivars to 6 feet tall or more.

Plant rhizomes in spring when soil has warmed, 3 to 4 inches deep, and depending on cultivar, 1 to 3 feet apart. Watch for snail and slug damage.

Where cannas are hardy, divide the plants every three or four years. You can also propagate them by sowing seed in warm soil (about 70° F) in the garden or in a pot. Soak the seed first for 24 to 48 hours. They are about the size of a pea and hard, hence their common name, Indian shot.

In the fall, cut back the tops of the plants to the ground when they freeze. Where temperatures don't fall below 20° F, cannas generally naturalize and can be left in the ground. In colder areas, lift the rhizomes in fall and store them in peat or vermiculite at 41° to 50° F.

Canna foliage is beautiful even when the plants are not in bloom. Dramatic variegated leaves unfurl all summer long.

USES: In borders, containers
SOIL: Any rich, organic, well-drained soil
CARE: Water and fertilize throughout the growing season
LIGHT: Sun
HARDINESS: Zones 7–10

Bright yellow-and-green-striped 'Pretoria' seems to capture the sunlight in the garden. Orange zinnias and deep blue salvia are bold complements .

Canna flowers appear at the top of tall stems, like a plume on a cap. The flowers attract hummingbirds.

Canna foliage can be many colors. This is 'Durban'.

Leaves also can have subtle stripes, like this 'Stuttgart'.

The mahogany foliage of 'Wyoming' is dramatic.

Tiger-striped leaves are a feature of 'Pretoria'.

CHIONODOXA

Glory-of-the-snow

- Lily family
- True bulb; deciduous
- Blooms late winter or early spring

Glory-of-the-snow is a native of the high mountain meadows of Turkey. It thrives where winters are cold, taking temperatures as low as minus 30° F. The plant blooms early, and it is adaptable to a wide range of conditions.

Plants naturalize in clumps and drifts, making these these charming little flowers especially suitable for informal gardens. You can also force the bulbs for midwinter bloom indoors.

USES: In woodlands, meadows, beds
SOIL: Most well-drained garden soils
CARE: Water during period of growth; not attractive to birds and squirrels
LIGHT: Sun; light shade in hot climates
HARDINESS: Zones 3–7

Plant bulbs 5 inches deep and about 2 inches apart in early fall. In containers, plant 12 to 15 bulbs per 8-inch pot.

Propagate bulbs by offsets in early fall or by sprinkling ripe seeds around the garden. If you plant glory-of-the-snow at the top of a slope, it will cover the entire hill in a few years by self-seeding.

In the lawn, glory-of-the-snow flowers early in a sweeping wave of color. In clusters in flower beds, they provide bright spots before most other plants emerge. They do not compete with perennials once the perennials are up, and late frosts rarely harm them.

Chionodoxa forbesii varies in height from 3 to 6 inches and includes varieties with white-eyed blue or pink flowers, about 1 inch wide, 6 to 10 per stem. *C. luciliae* has two or three white, blue, or pink flowers on each stem. *C. sardensis* is similar in appearance, with solid lavender-blue flowers on 4- to 6-inch stems.

Glory-of-the-snow blooms in early spring. Shown here is **Chionodoxa forbesii**, *which has a bright white eye.*

CLIVIA MINIATA

Clivia

- Amaryllis family
- Bulbous root; evergreen
- Blooms late winter or spring

Clivias are one of the brightest and longest-lasting flowers for indoors. In frost-free areas, they can illuminate shady garden corners.

They are amazingly undemanding. One division planted in a 12-inch pot will bloom and multiply prolifically for 10 years or more before it needs repotting.

Clivias flower in late winter or early spring when grown indoors. The blossoms are an umbel of 12 to 20 flowers at the top of each 12- to 18-inch stalk. They typically last for

USES: As houseplants, in borders
SOIL: Well drained, organic, acid to neutral
CARE: Water and fertilize during active growth; afterward, water sparingly
LIGHT: Partial to deep shade
HARDINESS: Zones 9–10

weeks and are soft orange with yellowish centers. Scarlet, deep red, salmon, and yellow forms are also sometimes available. Deep green, straplike leaves grow to about 2 feet long.

Clivias are South African natives. They are members of the amaryllis family, although their bulb looks nothing like that of an amaryllis.

Plant bulbs in fall or spring. Cover the fleshy roots with just a shallow layer of soil. The white part of the stem should be almost buried. Leave the plants in their pots as long as possible, dividing them only when the plants become overcrowded.

Protect clivias from nighttime temperatures below freezing and from direct sun, which burns the leaves. If plants spend the summer in the garden, bright, indirect light is best. Clivias are easily propagated by division, as well as by fresh seed sown in a moist medium kept at 80° to 85° F.

The most widely available species is *C. miniata*. The stunning yellow-flowering variety is *C. miniata citrina*.

Clivias are easy to grow, and their strappy evergreen leaves are good-looking all year long.

COLCHICUM

Autumn crocus, Fall crocus, Meadow saffron

- Lily family
- Corm; deciduous
- Blooms in fall

Autumn crocus grows from an odd-shaped corm. The flowers are sometimes already open when you buy the corms. They'll continue blooming after you plant them.

USES: In meadows, woodlands, beds
SOIL: Any well-drained garden soil
CARE: Water during period of active growth; deer and rodent proof
LIGHT: Partial shade or full sun
HARDINESS: Zones 4–9
BE AWARE: Corms are poisonous

Don't confuse autumn crocus with true crocuses, some of which also bloom in fall. It belongs to a different family. However, that's where any significant difference between the species ends. Like true crocuses, autumn crocus provides a low burst of brilliance in the fall garden.

Planted informally in clumps or broad drifts, this 4- to 6-inch-tall native of the Mediterranean region and parts of Asia

blooms in dazzling patches of amethyst, mauve, pink, rose, violet, purple, or white. Each corm produces several 2- to 8-inch-wide flowers. Flowering lasts for several weeks, or up to two months if several species are planted together in the garden.

Autumn crocus flowers bloom in the fall long before the leaves appear in late winter or early spring. The lush leaves grow to about 1 foot high, then die back after a few weeks. Plant them with spring-blooming daffodils and tulips, and you'll hardly notice the colchicum leaves. They fade about the same time as the foliage of spring-flowering bulbs.

Autumn crocus corms are often in bud or even in bloom when they arrive at garden shops in the early fall. Corms will even bloom on a tabletop or windowsill, but they will not live for long out of the soil.

Plant dormant corms in late summer or early fall, under 3 to 4 inches of soil, 6 to 9 inches apart. Plant blooming corms with the flowers a few inches above the soil line.

Propagate plants by division or by removing cormlets during the dormant period in early summer. Divide plants only when they become crowded. Autumn crocus will not naturalize in frost-free areas; they need some winter cold.

The following are some of the most beautiful members of this genus. Buy them as soon as they are available in the fall and plant immediately. They'll bloom within weeks.

Autumn crocus (*C. autumnale*) bears a profusion of medium-size flowers. The white form 'Album' has a fine, ghostly presence in the fall garden. It is hardy to minus 20° F.

Byzantine colchicum (*C. byzantinum*) bears bright mauve flowers on white stems. A purple-tinged white form is also available. This is perhaps the best colchicum for growing in saucers of pebbles or on a windowsill. It is hardy to zone 6.

Showy colchicum (*C. speciosum*) is the largest and most popular colchicum. 'Album' is pure white, but hard to find. 'Lilac Wonder' is amethyst-violet with white lines in the center.

Colchicum agrippinum has medium-size, star-shaped, violet-amethyst flowers checkered with white. It naturalizes rapidly where winters do not fall below minus 10° F.

Be aware that autumn crocus corms are poisonous if eaten.

BULBS FOR FALL

When garden centers receive their shipments of spring-blooming bulbs in early September, you'll often find among them a small collection of autumn crocuses, spider lilies, lily-of-the-field, and other fall-blooming species.

It's easy to overlook these bulbs among the bright displays of tulips and daffodils, but fall-blooming bulbs are beautiful in the autumn landscape and easy to grow. Every garden ought to have a few.

COLCHICUM

Colchicums, often called autumn crocuses, are among the most widely available of the fall-blooming bulbs.

Plant a few around fading hostas, in front of the spiky foliage of irises, or along the front walk where they make bright, cheerful displays on dreary fall days.

Don't rake autumn leaves off the garden where fall bulbs are emerging. Let them come up through the leaves. The contrast between the leaves and the violet, lilac, pink, or white flowers is striking, a perfect combination for the season.

SPIDER LILIES

In late September and early October, the spidery, red flowers of spider lily (*Lycoris radiata*) shoot out of the soil on stems about a foot tall. These spider lilies love the light shade of a woodland. In the South, they colonize around the drip lines of majestic old oaks.

TRUE CROCUS

Perhaps the most famous fall-blooming crocus is the saffron crocus (*Crocus sativus*). Its long, brilliant red stigmas are dried and sold as saffron. Showy crocus (*C. speciosus*) is the first to bloom, and one of the most prolific. *C. goulimyi* also blooms in early fall. Its pale purple flowers look like tiny wine goblets in the garden.

LILY-OF-THE-FIELD

This spectacular flower (*Sternbergia lutea*) looks like a golden-yellow crocus. Lily-of-the-field blooms prolifically in bright sun, forming a pool of gold in the garden. The flowers last for about two weeks. Plants do best in warm summers.

Spider lily flowers appear in early fall in pink or scarlet.

Fall-blooming true crocus is easy to grow and flowers for weeks.

Lily-of-the-field glows among a blue-flowering ground cover.

The magnificent leaves of elephant's ear can be two or three feet long.

COLOCASIA ESCULENTA

Elephant's ear

- Arum family
- Tuber; evergreen in frost-free areas
- Grown for its foliage

Elephant's ear is one of the most imposing of garden plants. Gardeners grow it not for its flowers but for its enormous velvety green leaves, which rise up on 3- to 7-foot stems.

The plant is a dramatic, sculptural, and fast-growing addition to any garden. Even in climates where you must dig the tubers and store them over the winter, elephant's ear can tower over the garden. It also thrives in large tubs, at least 10-inches in diameter.

This species has been cultivated as a food crop for more than 10,000 years. The tubers of this tropical Asian native are a staple in the diet of millions of people from India to the South Pacific. However, they are poisonous unless prepared properly.

USES: In borders, containers, bog gardens
SOIL: Rich, organic; tolerates wet, even standing water
CARE: Water generously and fertilize regularly; deer and rodent proof
LIGHT: Sun or light shade
HARDINESS: Zones 9–11

Start the tubers as you would those of caladium, and store them similarly (see page 43). Plant the tubers in spring 2 to 3 inches deep and up to 6 feet apart. For a longer display in most parts of the country, you can start the tubers indoors in spring, four to six weeks before night temperatures reach 60° F.

Grow elephant's ear in full sun in cool northern climates. A partly shaded spot is better along the Gulf Coast where tubers can be left in the ground all year round.

Deep green foliage is typical of elephant's ear, but there are about six species, some with dark purple or variegated leaves and some with purple stems. 'Fontanesia' has deep violet stems. 'Black Magic' has plum-purple leaves.

Lily-of-the-valley spreads to become a dense ground cover. The charming, fragrant, bell-shaped flowers have delicately scalloped edges.

CONVALLARIA MAJALIS

Lily-of-the-valley

- Lily family
- Rhizome; deciduous
- Blooms late spring

Lily-of-the-valley is universally valued for its delicate beauty and incomparable fragrance.

This native of the deciduous woodlands of the world's northern temperate zones is a perennial even where winters are cold and snowy. It is hardy to minus 40° F. Its leaves emerge in spring at the same time as daffodils.

The nodding bell-shaped flowers last for only a few weeks, but the attractive, dark green foliage persists throughout summer. Most lilies-of-the-valley have pure white single flowers, but there is also a pink cultivar, a double-flowered form, and even one with variegated leaves. Lily-of-the-valley is a traditional flower in wedding bouquets and is a fine cut flower.

Where lilies-of-the-valley are happy—in woodland gardens or shady flower beds—they spread quickly to form a dense ground cover. As a ground cover, in late spring, the

USES: In woodlands, borders, containers, as cut flowers
SOIL: Rich, organic
CARE: Water regularly year-round; fertilize in fall after the first frost; deer and rodent proof
LIGHT: Shade or partial shade
HARDINESS: Zones 3–7

fragrant flowers can perfume an entire corner of the garden.

Lily-of-the-valley grows from pips (single rhizomes with growth buds). Plant them in spring or fall. Because it can be invasive, plant lily-of-the-valley where it can spread with abandon or where a sidewalk or driveway can contain it. Set the pips 2 to 4 inches apart and 3 inches deep and water well. Mulch pips in fall.

Propagate lily-of-the-valley by dividing plants in fall into smaller clumps or single pips. Replant them immediately.

To force lily-of-the-valley for winter bloom, dig up a few pips after at least two months of cold weather. Or store bare pips in a plastic bag in the refrigerator for eight weeks. Then, plant the pips in a pot, barely covering them with soil and put them in a warm place.

CORYDALIS

Fumewort

- Fumitory family
- Rhizome or tuber; deciduous
- Blooms in spring

This native of European and Asian woodlands is related to Dutchman's-breeches and bleeding heart. It produces 3- to 9-inch stems of small tubular flowers, ranging from white or creamy gray to yellow to purple, rose, or lilac. Flowers rise over low mounds of blue-green, ferny leaves. Until a few years ago, corydalis was hard to find.

The pale rose-flowered fumewort (*Corydalis solida*) and yellow corydalis (*C. lutea*), which most nurseries sell as perennial plants, are among the most commonly available species

USES: In woodlands, borders
SOIL: Well drained, organic
CARE: Water regularly during growth and bloom; deer and pest resistant
LIGHT: Sun or light shade
HARDINESS: Zones 4–8

and are perhaps the easiest to grow, but blue-flowering varieties are also popular.

Blue corydalis (*C. flexuosa*) 'Blue Panda', from China, blooms from spring through frost in moist, shady woodland gardens. Another cultivar, 'Pere David', spreads vigorously.

There are at least two North American native species. Rock harlequin (*C. sempervirens*) has tiny pink and yellow flowers and occasionally is available as seed. It can be invasive. Pink-flowering *C. scouleri* is native to the Pacific Northwest.

Plant tubers 3 inches deep and 4 or 5 inches apart in fall. Fumewort purchased as plants should be put in the garden in spring. Protect them from sun while they become established.

Fumewort can be an ephemeral plant in many gardens. If the plants disappear shortly after flowers fade, mark the spot and look for them the following spring; they may merely have an extended dormancy in your yard.

Fumewort has soft, ferny foliage and small clusters of flowers. This is yellow corydalis. Blue-flowered forms also are available.

CRINUM

Milk-and-wine lily

- Amaryllis family
- True bulb; deciduous
- Blooms spring, summer, or fall

Milk-and-wine lilies are from warm regions, including the southeastern United States, South America, the Caribbean, South Africa, and tropical Asia. This imposing bulb somewhat resembles its cousin, *Amaryllis belladonna*. It produces lilylike white, pink, reddish, or bicolored flowers in loose clusters atop thick stalks up to 4 feet tall. Most have a spicy fragrance, and the plants' long arching leaves form large clumps.

USES: In borders, containers, as houseplants
SOIL: Well drained to moist, deep, organic
CARE: Water and fertilize during growth and flowering; unattractive to deer, rodents
LIGHT: Sun or light shade
HARDINESS: Zones 8–11

Milk-and-wine lilies are traditionally used in borders and tubs in the southeastern United States. Dense clumps in old gardens still bloom prolifically.

Spring is the best time to buy and plant milk-and-wine lilies. Set bulbs with their noses even with the soil, 12 to 36 inches apart. Where they are hardy, bulbs can be left undisturbed in the garden for years. Mulch them for winter protection if necessary.

In containers, plant bulbs in pots 2 inches larger in diameter than the bulb. The bulb's neck should be exposed above the soil. Where winters are cold, keep pots in a frost-free (35° to 45° F) place all winter.

Crinum bulbispermum, from South Africa, bears up to 20 flowers in the summer. Flowers will be either pink or they'll be white inside and red on the outside. Plants are 2 to 4 feet tall.

C. × *powellii*, a hybrid of *C. bulbispermum*, has umbels of up to 15 rose-pink, fragrant flowers. It is a little hardier than the species. 'Album' is a white form.

Milk-and-wine lilies form thick clumps in the garden in warm climates. Elsewhere, grow them in pots.

Crocuses spread easily in the lawn, creating sparkling colonies. These richly colored blooms are bright, spring-flowering Dutch crocus.

CROCUS

Crocus

- Iris family
- Corm; deciduous
- Blooms early spring, or fall, depending on species

USES: Meadows, rock gardens, borders, woodlands, containers
SOIL: Well drained
CARE: Water regularly during season of growth and flowering; attractive to deer and rodents
LIGHT: Sun or light shade
HARDINESS: Zones 3–7

Spring-blooming crocus can be relied upon to provide the first spots of color in the garden. There are about 80 crocus species native to the Mediterranean area, but most crocuses sold today are Dutch hybrids.

Crocus flowers are 2 to 4 inches tall with cup-shaped or flaring blooms right at ground level. The flowers can be white, blue, purple, lavender, yellow, or gold. Some are bicolored. Grasslike foliage appears either before, with, or after the flowers, depending on the species.

Where well adapted, most crocuses spread freely and are at their showiest when grouped in clusters of 10 to 25 bulbs.

Plant spring-blooming crocuses in fall; fall-blooming crocus (see p. 49) in early fall. Set corms 5 inches deep and 2 to 3 inches apart in the garden, or 1 inch deep in a pot, seven to nine corms per 5-inch pot.

Crocus flowers open wide on sunny days and close up again when the weather is cold or cloudy.

Where squirrels are a problem, plant corms a bit deeper than usual, tamp soil down firmly, water well, and immediately mulch with 2 inches of chopped autumn leaves. After crocuses are well established, squirrels rarely will bother them.

Two popular spring-blooming types are snow crocus, (*C. chrysanthus*), which

CROCUSES IN THE LAWN

Crocus corms are so small that they can be wedged into the garden nearly anywhere—in flower beds, around bases of trees, and even in spaces between paving stones. They especially make a fine display growing in the lawn. Crocuses bloom before the mowing season begins and won't interfere with the care and maintenance of a healthy lawn.

To plant crocus in a lawn, use a trowel with a narrow blade or a Korean trowel, which has a curved blade shaped like a miniature plow. Stab through the grass with your tool to make a hole and insert a crocus corm in every hole.

To plant a cloud of crocus corms, use a spade to cut out a thick square of turf, plant the corms in the soil, and set the turf patch back on top, tamping it down well with your foot. Or plant crocuses in a large ring to create a whimsical "fairy circle." After planting, water well.

In spring, crocuses come up through the grass. If you let foliage mature before mowing, your crocus display will multiply. Glory-of-the-snow, striped squill, windflower, and squill also grow well in lawns.

blooms early; and Dutch or giant crocus (*C. vernus* hybrids), which bloom later and have neon-bright, 4-inch flowers.

Crocus corms are small and hard with a netted tunic protecting them.

CROCOSMIA X CROCOSMIIFLORA

Montbretia

- Iris family
- Corm; deciduous
- Blooms summer and early fall

Montbretia is an old-fashioned favorite, native to central and southern Africa. Where winter temperatures are mild, it is one of the most care-free bulbs you can grow.

Montbretia foliage is narrow and swordlike and forms dense, spreading clumps. Thin, branching, 3- to 4-foot stems bear brilliant, 1- to 2-inch scarlet to orange flowers with up to 50 flowers on each stem. Flowers of some hybrids are even larger, up to 3 inches wide. In a vase indoors, the flowers last more than a week.

USES: In borders, meadows
SOIL: Any well-drained garden soil
CARE: Crocosmia is drought tolerant
LIGHT: Sun or light shade
HARDINESS: Zones 6–10 with protection

Most of the widely available montbretia are hybrids between two species (*Crocosmia aurea* and *C. pottsii*) and are known as Montbretia hybrids. The cultivar 'Lucifer' has deep red flowers and is the hardiest crocosmia. 'Emily McKenzie' has dark orange blossoms with a brownish red throat.

Plant the corms 3 to 5 inches deep and 6 to 8 inches apart after the last spring frost. Montbretia corms look very much like crocus corms, and apparently they smell like them, too, because squirrels will dig them up. Where squirrels are a problem, start the corms in pots and transplant into the garden after the foliage is well developed. Squirrels are less interested in the corms at this stage.

Where montbretia is only marginally hardy, it may survive the winter outdoors with a thick mulch of autumn leaves. Where it is not hardy, dig and store the corms in dry peat moss at 35° to 41° F. Propagate the plants by division in spring or fall.

Montbretia corms produce lush foliage and arching sprays of flowers that last for weeks in the garden.

CYCLAMEN

Cyclamen

- Primrose family
- Tuber; deciduous
- Bloom time is long but varies

The plants sold as florists cyclamen are one of several 8- to 12-inch-tall hybrids of *Cyclamen persicum*. They bear white, purple, red, pink, rose, salmon, or bicolored flowers. Their butterflylike flower buds rise from a mound of mottled, heart-shaped leaves.

Although it's a favorite houseplant, florists cyclamen can also be grown outdoors in spring through fall whenever temperatures

USES: As houseplants, in containers
SOIL: Well drained, organic
CARE: Water regularly but not excessively during growth and bloom
LIGHT: Indirect light, shade, partial shade
HARDINESS: Zones 9–11

are above freezing. In areas where temperatures do not drop below 20° F, florists cyclamen can be planted in the ground and left outdoors year round. Several other cyclamen species are hardy in colder areas (see page 91).

Florists cyclamen is usually sold as a potted plant. When buying one, look for many flower buds among the leaves.

Although the tubers for florists cyclamen are not offered for sale, seeds are. Sow them in a potting mix containing sand in late summer for bloom about 15 months later.

Keep the plants in a cool (55° F) spot with filtered light. Then, about a month before they're due to flower, increase the temperature to 65° F.

Established florists cyclamen needs a humid, cool environment. A room that is 60° to 65° F during the day and 40° to 50° F at night is suitable. Do not overwater plants. Repot them during dormancy. Set the tuber just at the surface of the soil and keep the soil barely moist until growth resumes in fall.

Florists cyclamen plants have twirling flowers rising above silver-splashed leaves. They are care-free houseplants.

Decorative dahlias have double flowers; some have twisted petals.

A variety of tall, flashy dahlias fills out this summer flower bed. Dahlias bloom for a month or more, usually until the first frost.

Collarette dahlias have a ruffle of petals around a yellow center.

Ball-shaped dahlias are bright globes of tight petals.

Cactus-flowered dahlia blooms are usually quite large and have many petals.

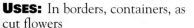

Dahlia

- Aster family
- Tuberous root; deciduous
- Blooms early summer to fall

From a couple of wild Mexican dahlias, hybridizers have created a staggering array of showy garden plants. Dahlias range in height from about 1 foot to 7 feet and bear flowers as small as buttons or large as dinner plates in a huge assortment of forms and colors. They can be grown anywhere in the United States but are hardy year-round only in warm climates. Perhaps more than any other flower, dahlias offer the perfect solution to the busy gardener's dilemma: lots of bright color throughout the summer without intricate planning and hard work. Dahlias are also cheerful cut flowers, lasting up to a week.

Dahlias thrive in well-drained soil in any sunny spot in the garden. In spring, plant tuberous roots, which look like clusters of sausages, setting the crown 3 inches below the soil. You'll recognize the crown by the new roots projecting from the collar at the base of the stem. As you plant, set sturdy stakes next to the roots of larger cultivars to avoid injuring them later. As shoots grow, fill in with 1 to 3 inches more soil.

Pinch shoot tips twice: first after three sets of leaves have developed and then again in a few weeks. Pinching delays flowering but helps establish a strong, bushy plant. Tie taller cultivars to their stakes with strips of cloth or nylon stocking. Fertilizing with a low-nitrogen formula is best because too much nitrogen creates a lot of foliage with few flowers.

USES: In borders, containers, as cut flowers
SOIL: Well drained, sandy, organic, acid to neutral
CARE: Water and fertilize during the growing season; deer and rodent resistant
LIGHT: Sun; midday shade in hot areas
HARDINESS: Zones 8–11

Seedlings of dwarf dahlias are often available from garden shops in the spring. Plant them in the garden as soon as it is warm. Dwarf or patio dahlias fit nicely in window boxes, in pots, or at the front of flower beds. Taller dahlias may be planted as the centerpiece of a tub or large container, or toward the middle or back of flower beds. In the garden, dahlias need watering during dry spells. Plants in pots may need water every day during hot weather. They should start to bloom about midsummer.

Where temperatures drop below 10° F, dig and store clumps or individual tubers in dry sand or vermiculite. Do not wash tubers before storing; it promotes rot. Instead brush soil off. And be careful not to break or cut tubers unnecessarily. Dry tubers for a day and store them in shallow trays where the temperature is about 40° F. The tubers will shrivel if they are too warm or too dry during storage. Divide the clumps in spring; include part of the old stem in each division.

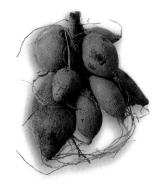

Dahlia tubers are fragile. Handle them carefully.

ERANTHIS

Winter aconite

- Buttercup family
- Tuber; deciduous
- Blooms winter or early spring

Winter aconite is one of the earliest bulbs to bloom. Even before the first crocus flowers emerge, drifts or clumps of winter aconite push through the mulch to break winter's somber mood.

Each stem is topped by a yellow, upward-facing flower, like a large buttercup, sitting on a ruff of foliage. Winter aconites open in the sun, and on cloudy days stay closed like big yellow beads scattered in the garden. Winter

USES: In borders, woodlands, containers
SOIL: Well drained, organic, neutral to alkaline
CARE: Provide year-round moisture; deer and rodent resistant
LIGHT: Full to partial shade
HARDINESS: Zones 3–7

aconites need winter temperatures at least as low as 20° F and are hardy to minus 30° F. Where well adapted, it spreads by seeding itself, looking as much at home under a tree in the garden as in the wild woodlands of its native Europe and Asia.

Plant tubers promptly upon receiving them in late summer or early fall. Plant them 5 inches deep and 1 to 2 inches apart. Winter aconites only grow 3 to 6 inches tall, so plant them in conspicuous places. They glow under the branches of deciduous shrubs or just in front of daffodils along a path. They last up to a month and may overlap snowdrops and crocus—good planting companions. After winter aconite flowers fade, allow the seeds to ripen, and scratch them into the soil. Seedlings take two to three years to bloom.

The most commonly sold species are *Eranthis cilicica* and *E. hyemalis*. Both have yellow flowers; the foliage of *E. cilicia* is bronze as it emerges and turns green as it matures.

Winter aconites bloom in late winter. The flowers open when the sun is out and stay tightly closed on cloudy days.

EREMURUS

Foxtail lily
Desert candle

- Lily family
- Rhizomatous root; deciduous
- Blooms late spring or early summer

Foxtail lily is one of the most spectacular bulbs for sunny gardens. Hundreds of small white or pastel blooms cover the upper half of each dense, bottlebrush-shaped spike that rises 3 to 7 feet above fountains of strappy foliage. Foxtail lily is a superb, dramatic cut flower that may last several weeks.

Native to western and central Asia, foxtail lily's tuberous roots look like a cross between

USES: Borders, meadows, cut flowers
SOIL: Well drained, organic, sandy, acid to neutral
CARE: Give ample water during growing season; deer and rodent resistant
LIGHT: Sun
HARDINESS: Zones 5–7

an octopus and a starfish. They need gentle handling. Plant them in early fall immediately after purchase. Do not allow them to dry out.

Dig a hole large enough to accommodate setting the crown on a mound of soil. Space roots so they can spread without crowding. Crowns should be 4 to 6 inches deep.

Do not disturb these plants unnecessarily. The foliage dies in summer, so mark the plants' position to avoid injuring them while dormant. Propagate foxtail lily by lifting and dividing old plants when their crowns grow up and out of the soil.

Shelford and Ruiter hybrids, both cultivars of *Eremurus isabellinus*, come in a range of colors, from white to pink, yellow, orange, and cream. *E. stenophyllus* from southwestern Asia, bears 2- to 3-foot spikes of yellow or golden yellow flowers. *E. himalaicus* from the Himalayas grows 4 to 8 feet tall and has white flowers. *E. robustus* may reach 6 to 10 feet tall and has deep pink flowers.

Flower spikes of foxtail lilies can grow up to 4 feet tall in the garden. They bloom in late spring and need strong sunlight to grow well.

A colony of pink-flowering dog's-tooth violets brightens a woodland in spring.

ERYTHRONIUM

Dog's-tooth violet, Trout lily, Adder's tongue

- Lily family
- Corm; deciduous
- Blooms in spring

Erythroniums are woodland garden gems. Of the 15 or so species, most are North American natives. They thrive at woodland edges and in shady flower beds.

Despite their delicate appearance, dog's-tooth-violets are hardy bulbs. They willingly colonize an area with little attention from the gardener.

All of the species, whether native to North America, Europe, or Asia, are similar in form with one or more gracefully nodding lily-shaped blossoms per plant. The flower stems are enclosed by pairs of folded, often beautifully mottled leaves. Flower colors vary from white to cream, yellow, pink, or purple. All grow best where the ground freezes during the winter.

USES: In woodlands, borders, containers
SOIL: Well drained, organic
CARE: Water during period of growth and bloom
LIGHT: Light to medium shade
HARDINESS: Zones 3–8

Plant corms as early as possible in fall, immediately after purchase. Do not let them dry out. Set them 4 or 5 inches deep and 3 to 5 inches apart. It is not necessary to water during the summer, but mulch their growing area to conserve moisture. Allow seedpods to ripen and fall around the plants. Seedlings will bloom in two or three years. Move the plants only when they become crowded.

Dog's-tooth violet (*Erythronium dens-canis*), a variety from Europe and Asia, has white or rose to purple flowers with blue anthers. The "dog's-tooth violet" common name refers to the shape of this species' corms.

Mahogany trout lily (*E. revolutum*), native to British Columbia and California, has rose-pink flowers with yellow bands on the inner sides of the petals. A popular cultivar 'Pagoda' has sulphur yellow flowers with a brown ring in the center and lightly mottled leaves.

Pineapple lily's flowers bloom along stalks up to 2 feet tall. A tuft of green leaves at the top of the stalks makes the plant look like a pineapple.

EUCOMIS

Pineapple lily

- Lily family
- True bulb; deciduous
- Blooms in summer and sometimes at other seasons

This South African native is easy to grow indoors or in gardens where temperatures stay above 10° F. Plants are especially striking when growing in pots.

The pineapple lily's common name comes from the appearance of the flower spikes. Each dense spike of blooms is crowned by tufts of small leaves—the "pineapple." Flowers last for several weeks, and the impressive spikes make excellent cut flowers. Some species have fragrant flowers.

Plants grow to about 2 feet tall and have broad, straplike basal leaves that arch in a fountain shape. Some species have wavy edges on the leaves.

In March, plant the bulbs about 5 inches deep. Plant several bulbs together in pots.

USES: In borders, containers, as houseplants
SOIL: Well drained, sandy, organic
CARE: Water generously and fertilize lightly during growth and bloom; attractive to deer and rodents
LIGHT: Full sun to light shade
HARDINESS: Zones 7–11

Once growth begins, start watering and feeding regularly. Keep soil moist while plants are growing, dry when they are dormant. Although pineapple lily grows in full sun, plants do best when they are lightly shaded during the heat of the day.

Where winters are cold, dig up bulbs or move pots to a warm (55° to 68° F) place for the winter. Allow bulbs to dry before storing. As to division, plants are happy to remain undisturbed year after year.

Eucomis autumnalis has wavy-edged leaves and green flowers. *E. bicolor* has purple-edged, rather pale green flowers. *E. comosa* has purple spots on the undersides of the leaves and green, white, pinkish, or purplish flowers.

FREESIA

Freesia

- Iris family
- Corm; deciduous
- Blooms in spring

Freesia, a South African native, bears elegant flowers on slender, curved spikes above fans of small gladioluslike leaves. It is among the most beautifully fragrant flowers. Trumpet-shaped blooms to 2 inches long are white, yellow, gold, orange, pink, red, purple, or violet. Many are bicolored and beautifully veined or feathered; some are double.

USES: In borders, containers, as houseplants, cut flowers
SOIL: Well drained, sandy
CARE: Water regularly and fertilize lightly during growth and flowering; attractive to deer and rodents
LIGHT: Full sun or very light shade
HARDINESS: Zones 9–10

Cut flowers last more than a week.

Freesias grow 12 to 18 inches tall. In gardens where the temperature doesn't drop below 20° F and where summers are dry and winters cool and moist, freesias are perennial.

In the South, plant corms in the garden in fall, pointed ends up, 5 inches deep and 1 or 2 inches apart. Plant them in spring in the North. Stagger plantings for extended bloom, which begins 10 to 12 weeks after planting. In pots, set corms 1 inch deep, six to eight per 6-inch pot. Water plants while they grow but do not overwater.

Freesias sprawl, so set plants close together for support, and stake them as needed. They prefer daytime temperatures in the 60° to 70° F range, dropping to 50° to 60° F at night. In hot areas, they will go dormant in summer. In areas with wet summers, dig and store corms dry at 77° to 86° F for at least three months. Store pots in a dry spot until fall.

Clusters of luminous freesia flowers turn their faces up at the ends of arching stems. The flowers are sweetly fragrant.

FRITILLARIA

Fritillary, Checkered lily, Crown imperial

- Lily family
- True bulb; deciduous
- Blooms in spring

This diverse genus, native to the Northern Hemisphere, has long been prized by gardeners. Some of the flowers grow up to 4 feet tall while others are subtle plants for woodland gardens. All have bell- or cuplike flowers, usually nodding, with a shiny reservoir of nectar near the inner base of the

USES: In borders, meadows, woodlands, containers
SOIL: Well drained, organic
CARE: Water regularly; reduce water when plants die back after blooming; deer and rodent resistant
LIGHT: Full sun or light shade, depending on species.
HARDINESS: Zones 3–7

petals. Garden shops seem to carry a greater variety of fritillary every year.

Plant bulbs in fall immediately after purchase, 5 inches deep and 2 inches apart. Do not allow the bulbs to dry out before planting and be careful not to damage their fleshy scales. Plant them on their sides so the fall rains won't collect in the bulbs and rot them.

Crown imperial (*Fritillaria imperialis*) is the largest and most widely grown fritillary. A 2- to 4-foot stem rises from a whorl of glossy leaves to form a cluster of orange, red, or yellow flowers capped by a dense tuft of small leaves. It may need staking. Some people object to its musky odor.

Checkered lily (*F. meleagris*), also called snake's head and guinea-hen flower, bears one to three bell-shaped, checked, and veined flowers from deep brown to rosy lilac, wine, even white. It is suited to borders, meadows, and bright woodlands with rich, moist soil.

Persian fritillary (*F. persica*), from the Middle East, produces up to 30 deep violet to reddish-purple blossoms on 2- to 3-foot stems.

The charming bell-shaped flowers of the checkered lily dangle from slender, grassy stems. They invite close inspection, so plant bulbs near paths and in front of borders.

A well-established planting of snowdrops may produce dozens of snow white flowers. Allow them a few years to grow into dense clumps.

GALANTHUS

Snowdrop

- Amaryllis family
- True bulb; deciduous
- Blooms late winter to early spring

USES: In mixed borders, meadows, woodlands, containers
SOIL: Cool, moist
CARE: Water through bloom period; deer and rodent proof
LIGHT: Light shade
HARDINESS: Zones 3–9

Fragrant snowdrops are among the first flowers of the spring, often pushing up through the snow. Three or four plants are enough to make a quiet but cheerful statement. Large, naturalized plantings will lift your heart at the end of winter.

Snowdrops are native to the deciduous woods of Europe and Turkey. They spread in cool woodland conditions where winter lows reach at least 20° F but are not colder than minus 30° F.

Plant bulbs 3 to 4 inches deep and 2 to 3 inches apart in the fall. They can be difficult to establish and may take a couple of years to settle into the garden.

The surest way to propagate snowdrops is to divide clumps as soon as foliage begins to turn yellow in spring. Each division should contain four or five bulbs. Replant them immediately after dividing.

To force the flowers for bloom indoors, plant bulbs in the fall 1 inch deep, putting about four bulbs in a 4-inch pot. Place the pot in a cold frame or unheated greenhouse. When buds begin to develop, bring the pots out to a very cool but bright spot indoors. After they bloom, plant the bulbs in the garden while the foliage is still green.

Giant snowdrop (*Galanthus elwesii*) grows 6 to 10 inches tall and bears nodding 1½-inch flowers with pure white, rounded outer petals and slightly green inner petals. This species withstands hot weather better than the next.

Common snowdrops (*G. nivalis*) bloom a bit earlier than giant snowdrops and are smaller and daintier with 1-inch flowers on 6-inch stems. Many varieties are available. 'Flore Pleno' has double flowers.

Summer hyacinth presents its flowers on tall spikes in late summer. This is green summer hyacinth with pale green blooms.

GALTONIA

Summer hyacinth

- Lily family
- True bulb; deciduous
- Blooms in summer

USES: In borders, containers, as cut flowers
SOIL: Well drained, sandy, organic
CARE: Water during growth and bloom; deer and rodent resistant
LIGHT: Sun or light shade
HARDINESS: Zones 6–10

This South African native deserves greater popularity. It is a choice flower both for garden beds and containers.

Summer hyacinth vaguely resembles a stretched out Dutch hyacinth. It bears up to 30 elegant white, nodding, fragrant flowers on sturdy 2- to 4-foot-tall spikes. The blossoms are first-rate cut flowers, lasting more than a week in a bouquet.

Summer hyacinths are easy to grow. In warm areas, plant bulbs in fall; elsewhere, wait until spring to put them out. Set the bulbs in holes 6 to 9 inches deep.

The strappy foliage of summer hyacinth grows to about 2 feet tall, so give these plants plenty of room to spread out. Although summer hyacinth does well in pots, it does not like to be crowded.

On the northern edge of its hardiness zone, summer hyacinth may survive being left in the garden over winter if it is well protected by a thick mulch of autumn leaves or other organic mulch. Snails and slugs can be a problem, though, so be sure to remove the mulch as soon as growth begins to emerge in spring.

Summer hyacinth (*Galtonia candicans*) has leaves up to three feet long and flower spikes up to 4 feet. Its blossoms are white with a green tinge. It is hardy in zones 6 to 9.

Green summer hyacinth (*G. viridiflora*) has pale green flowers and blue-green leaves.

GLADIOLUS

Gladiolus

- Iris family
- Corm; deciduous
- Blooms in spring, summer, or fall

There are thousands of varieties of common gladiolus (*Gladiolus × hortulanus*). They bloom in an astonishing array of colors—everything except for blue—and may be bi- and tricolored.

Flowers can be 6 inches across. But miniature hybrids and species have smaller flowers than tall glads. All make long-lasting cut flowers with a vase life of one to two weeks. Cut the flower spike when the first bud at the base of the spike opens.

Because of their height (to 5 or 6 feet) and slenderness, gladiolas are suited to growing in large clumps rather than in straight lines. For greatest impact, plant one variety per group, placing larger types at the back of the bed.

USES: In flower beds, containers, as cut flowers
SOIL: Well drained, sandy, organic
CARE: Water regularly during growth and bloom; attractive to deer and rodents
LIGHT: Full sun
HARDINESS: Zones 7–10

Gladiolus flowers open from the bottom up along tall flower stems. Strong plants produce two dozen or more flowers on a single stem.

Plant the corms in spring, 4 to 6 inches deep and 4 to 6 inches apart. In areas with hot summers, plant them in winter so they will bloom before the summer's heat takes over.

Glads take 60 to 100 days to bloom after planting. Speed them along with fertilizer. As you plant the corms, thoroughly mix bulb fertilizer into the planting hole. Apply a low-nitrogen fertilizer a month after planting and again when spikes begin to develop.

Protect gladiolus from wind by growing them near a hedge, which acts as a windbreak. Or stake their stems. Planting corms deep also helps.

Watch for signs of thrips: washed-out, streaked leaves and distorted flowers. Buying healthy corms and keeping plants healthy are your best insurance against these pests. Thrips insecticides are also available.

In the fall, dig the corms and store them uncovered in a well-ventilated, cool spot. Or, leave them in place in areas where they are hardy.

Byzantine gladiolus (*G. communis byzantinus*) has magenta-flowers. It tends to be hardier than garden hybrids.

Gladiolus corms may be up to 1½ inches around and slightly pointed. Roots grow from the flat side.

Sword-like gladiolus foliage is dense enough to create a background for other flowers, and the spikes draw the eye up through a garden's levels of bloom. In windy places, it is a good idea to stake plants.

Gloriosa lilies have wiry stems and exotic flowers. Leaf tendrils allow them to cling to a trellis.

GLORIOSA

Climbing lily, Flame lily, Gloriosa lily

- Lily family
- Tuber; deciduous vine
- Blooms late summer to fall

USES: As houseplants, in containers, on trellises
SOIL: Fast draining, organic, acid to neutral
CARE: Water and fertilize during early growth through bloom period; attractive to deer and rodents
LIGHT: Light to medium shade
HARDINESS: Zones 7–10

Gloriosa lilies have dramatic yellow-and-red flowers with petals that appear to have been flung back by a tropical wind. If you cut them just before petals bend back, the graceful 4- to 5-inch flowers last up to eight days in arrangements. Split the end of the main stem before putting it into a vase.

This South African member of the lily family is one of the few bulbs that grows as a vine. The plant's glossy leaves have tendrils at the tips, which wrap around supports to help plants easily climb trellises and other structures. Plants reach 8 feet tall.

In the garden, plant the fingerlike tubers after your zone's last frost. Set them in the hole horizontally 2 inches deep. For a longer bloom period outdoors, start the tubers indoors in late winter, then transplant them into the garden. An 8-inch pot will accommodate one to three tubers.

Gloriosa lily prefers 60° to 70° F night temperatures, 75° F plus during the day, and high humidity. It will tolerate night temperatures of 50° to 60° F.

After blooming, gradually cease watering, then dig and store the tubers dry for about six months at 50° to 60° F. You may leave them in pots of dry soil until spring. Repot them in fresh soil in spring. Propagate by offsets or divisions of the rhizome when repotting.

Gloriosa superba 'Rothschildiana' has yellow wavy-edged petals flushed with crimson. 'Lutea' has pure yellow flowers.

Amaryllis bulbs produce one or two flower stalks, each stalk with two to six dramatic trumpet-shaped blooms. They like to be crowded, so plant several bulbs in large pots.

HIPPEASTRUM

Amaryllis

- Amaryllis family
- True bulb; deciduous
- Blooms indoors winter or spring; outdoors, spring or summer

USES: In flower beds, containers, as houseplants
SOIL: Well drained, organic, sandy
CARE: Water sparingly during root growth in winter and regularly after foliage appears; attractive to deer and rodents
LIGHT: Full sun or light shade
HARDINESS: Zones 7–11

Hippeastrum's common name is amaryllis, but it should not be confused with *Amaryllis belladonna*, an entirely different plant.

Modern hybrid amaryllis varieties have bulbs that are almost as big as softballs. Most people grow them as winter-blooming houseplants.

The large bulbs should form two flower stalks in a season. Their sudden emergence from the bulbs, as well as the plants' rapid growth and showy blooms, make amaryllis very dramatic houseplants.

Plants bear two to six flowers atop each 12- to 36-inch-tall stalk. The striking 6- to 10-inch flowers come in shades of red, pink, salmon, green, yellow, or white and may also be bicolored or striped. Bold, straplike foliage may develop with the flower stalks or appear after flowering. Cut flowers last five to seven days.

To bring amaryllis into bloom indoors, plant one bulb per 6-inch pot with a third of the bulb showing above the pot rim. Place the pot in a 70° F room in bright light. For a long season of indoor bloom, stagger the plantings over a month or more.

In warm climates, where amaryllis are hardy, you can plant bulbs in the garden about 8 inches deep and at least 1 foot apart in winter or spring. For a longer bloom period outdoors, start the tubers in pots indoors in late winter, then transplant them to the garden. Where the climate is favorable, amaryllis will multiply willingly.

Amaryllis bulbs are susceptible to rot if overwatered.

HEMEROCALLIS

Daylily

- Lily family
- Tuberous roots; deciduous or evergreen
- Blooms late spring to fall

The numerous and widely sold hybrids of daylilies offer beauty, variety, and versatility and make few demands on the gardener. Most are descendants of plants from Europe and Asia, especially Japan. If mulched before winter sets in, they thrive throughout the United States, even in the coldest areas.

Daylilies bear blossoms up to 6 inches across. They range from the yellows, oranges, and tawny reds of old-fashioned favorites to a multitude of shades and bicolor combinations in cream, yellow, gold, red, pink, apricot, purple, violet, and plum. Yellow varieties are often fragrant. Clusters of flowers are held above gracefully arching 1- to 2-foot leaves.

The tallest varieties grow up to 5 feet high, the smallest only a foot or so. Daylilies can be planted as a ground cover in large gardens or used in perennial or mixed borders. Once established, they are tough plants, tolerant of drought and neglect.

Most plants bloom for about a month, although individual flowers last only a day. Choose cultivars that bloom at different times, and you can have daylily blossoms from late spring into early fall. Cultivars marked "early" bloom in late May or June, "midseason" varieties in July, and "late" ones in August or early September.

Daylilies are also useful as cut flowers. If you refrigerate them during the day, flowers will open in the evening.

Plant tuberous roots or nursery-grown plants anytime during the growing season, although spring or early fall is best. Set crowns close to the surface of the soil and space plants 1 to 3 feet apart.

Daylilies thrive in full sun or in light shade, but in the hottest climates their flowers look best with some shade. They accept virtually any well-drained soil. Propagate by division.

USES: In flower beds, containers, meadows
SOIL: Any well-drained garden soil
CARE: Plants bloom best with regular watering and occasional light applications of fertilizer; deer and rodent resistant
LIGHT: Full sun to partial shade
HARDINESS: Zones 3–10

DAYLILIES THAT BLOOM ALL SUMMER

Most daylilies are at their best in early summer, and the show is over after a few weeks of glorious bloom.

Although it is possible to extend the season with successive plantings or with different varieties, hybridizers in recent years have introduced a number of repeat-blooming varieties to make all that unnecessary. These daylilies come into bloom early; then after a short rest, they flower again, repeating the process so often they seem to be in almost constant bloom.

Some of the best of these reblooming varieties are 'Stella d'Oro', which has gold flowers; 'Happy Returns', extremely heat-tolerant and canary yellow; and 'Black-eyed Stella', which is golden yellow with a dark smudge in the center.

Clumps of daylilies shine in a summer garden. Each flower lasts only a day, but flower stalks bear many blooms. These daylilies are planted with dahlias, blue salvia, and bee balm.

Daylily's roots are vigorous with foliage emerging from the crowns in early spring.

A close look at 'Elmo Jackson' daylily reveals flowers with slightly ruffled edges and a pretty blend of colors. Some hybrids produce up to 50 buds on each flower stalk.

Ginger lily

- Ginger family
- Rhizome; evergreen or deciduous
- Blooms in late summer

Gingers give every garden a touch of tropical spice. Although they are exotic plants—most are from India and Malaysia—they adapt to hot summers in temperate gardens and produce spectacular flowers.

Ginger lilies, the hedychiums, are a group of about 50 species grown mainly for their lush ornamental foliage but especially for their heavily fragrant flowers, which bloom in clusters and resemble a cloud of butterflies. Be sure to plant ginger lily where you can enjoy the fragrance up close. The flowering period lasts for about six weeks, during which time they attract hummingbirds.

Where plants are hardy, gingers may grow enormous, up to 10 feet or even taller. Ginger lilies do best in rich, organic soil and prefer plenty of moisture. These plants thrive in shade and in warm, humid conditions. Where they are well adapted, full sun helps keep invasive growth under control.

Plant the rhizomes in spring with the bulbs' tips just below the surface and 24 inches apart.

Ginger lilies are a good choice for large containers. Plant them in heavy, wide pots (the plants are top heavy) and allow them to become crowded.

Fertilize ginger lilies lightly once or twice during the growing season but do not overfertilize. Water generously during dry periods and mulch to help retain moisture. A 2-inch layer of organic mulch also will protect the rhizomes during winter in areas where gingers are only marginally hardy.

Where winters are cold, dig the rhizomes immediately after the first frost and store them at 45° to 55° F. In warm areas, gingers can stay in the garden, but they may be deciduous during cool, dry periods. Cut back faded foliage of the deciduous types. New growth will sprout from the rhizome.

Butterfly ginger (*Hedychium coronarium*) has large, gardenia-like, intensely fragrant snow-white flowers. Its leaves look like a bouquet of giant feathers. It is considered the hardiest and easiest to grow of the ginger lilies and reaches 4 to 6 feet tall.

Kahili ginger (*H. gardnerianum*) has waxy leaves and fragrant yellow flowers with red stamens. Kahili ginger blooms earlier than butterfly ginger, tolerates full sun, and grows 5 to 6 feet tall.

Red-leaf ginger (*H. greenei*) has pale, red-orange flowers. The plants have dark stems and green foliage with a hint of red. They grow 3 to 4 feet tall in shade.

USES: In borders, containers
SOIL: Well drained, organic
CARE: Water generously
LIGHT: Part shade to full sun
HARDINESS: Zones 8–11

'Tara' Kahili ginger is native to the Himalayas.

Ginger lilies are dramatic, colorful plants that tower over a summer flower border. Where they are not hardy, grow them in pots.

Tropical flowers are seldom subtle. These red canna blooms seem to flash like traffic lights.

Caladium leaves often have dazzling patterns of variegation.

Rain beads up on the tough leaves of elephant's ears.

TROPICAL BULBS FOR SUMMER GARDENS

Cool, lush, foliage and bright, exotic, fragrant flowers are among the special pleasures of the tropical summer garden. You don't have to live in a tropical climate (or take a vacation in one) to enjoy such a garden. Some of the best tropical plants for temperate gardens are bulbs, including gingers of every description, lobster claw (*Heliconia*), elephant's ear, canna lilies, spider lilies, and caladiums. They are especially well suited to temperate gardens because they have a dormant period and can be dug up and stored for the winter without damage.

All tropical bulbs are too tender to survive year-round in the garden where freezes are frequent or extended. Wherever summers are hot, though, these plants can spend the season outdoors in the ground or in pots, and they will respond to summer's warmth with exuberant growth. Plant them where you will be able to appreciate their strikingly architectural foliage and where you can enjoy the fragrance of the varieties that flower.

You can also grow tropical plants as houseplants, but their large size often makes this a rather formidable undertaking. Both the flowers and foliage of tropical bulbs are excellent additions to an arrangement of summer flowers in a vase.

Mail-order specialists still offer the widest selection of tropical bulbs, but garden centers are stocking larger numbers of them every year.

HYMENOCALLIS

Peruvian daffodil
Crown beauty, Spider lily

- Amaryllis family
- True bulb; deciduous
- Blooms in summer

Peruvian daffodils are tender bulbs, native to tropical and subtropical areas of North and South America. Yet gardeners in every climate know them for their heavily fragrant, intricately formed flowers and broad, straplike leaves that stay green all summer. Peruvian daffodils make excellent cut flowers, lasting a week or longer.

Plant bulbs in the garden in spring or fall, about a foot apart. Cover them with about 4 inches of soil. Where winters are cold, plant Peruvian daffodils in spring, after nighttime temperatures reach 60° F.

In containers, plant one bulb per 8-inch pot, with the tip of the bulb just beneath the surface of the soil.

The white, spidery flowers of Peruvian daffodils grow in clusters on tall flower stalks.

USES: In borders, containers, damp gardens, as houseplants
SOIL: Well drained to moist, organic
CARE: Water generously; deer and rodent proof
LIGHT: Full sun or very light shade
HARDINESS: Zones 8–11

In frost-free areas where drainage is excellent, you can leave the bulbs in the ground. Elsewhere, dig them before frost or bring in pots of bulbs and store them at 60° to 70° F until spring. Allow container-grown plants to dry out once foliage has died back.

Propagate Peruvian daffodils from offsets in the fall. Seeds germinating in the garden will produce blooming plants in three or four years. Repot container plants every two years.

Basket flower (*H. narcissiflora*) is the most reliably hardy and widely available hymenocallis. A native of the Peruvian and Bolivian Andes, it bears four to six large, greenish-white flowers atop 2-foot stems. The flowers are fragrant at night. It is sometimes sold as *H. calathina* or *Ismene calathina*. 'Advance' has particularly durable flowers; 'Sulphur Queen' has primrose yellow flowers.

Hymenocallis × festalis is a hybrid of basket flower. It looks similar to basket flower but has narrower petals. Flowers are white.

HYACINTHOIDES

Spanish bluebell, Wood hyacinth

- Lily family
- True bulb; deciduous
- Blooms in spring

Relatives of hyacinths, Spanish bluebells (*Hyacinthoides hispanica*) are native to the woodlands of western Europe. They have loose, graceful spikes of bell-shaped blue, pink, or white blossoms, which are lovely cut and last up to a week. Plants grow 6 to 15 inches tall.

Spanish bluebells are adaptable plants, but they thrive best in rich, moist, organic soil in the bright shade of woodland gardens. They spread in clumps and drifts and lend themselves to growing in pots, especially when combined with daffodils, hyacinths, tulips, and crocuses.

At one time, Spanish bluebells were commonly called scilla. You may still find

Spanish bluebells need little attention from the gardener.

USES: In woodlands, borders, containers, meadows
SOIL: Well drained to moist, organic
CARE: Water regularly during growth and flowering; deer and rodent resistant
LIGHT: Partial shade or sun
HARDINESS: Zones 3–8

them sold under that name. Or you might also see them listed as endymion, another old species name.

Plant bulbs in the fall, 5 inches deep and 3 to 4 inches apart. You can also grow them in pots. Plant them 1 inch deep, with six or seven bulbs per 6-inch container. Propagate Spanish bluebells by division or by offsets.

Another species, Italian bluebell (*Hyacinthoides italica*), has fragrant lilac-blue flowers that appear on 1-foot spikes. English bluebell (*H. non-scripta*) bears fragrant, lilac-blue flowers on stems that grow up to 18 inches tall. White, blue, and pink forms are also available.

HYACINTHUS ORIENTALIS

Dutch hyacinth, Garden hyacinth

- Lily family
- True bulb; deciduous
- Blooms in spring

Hyacinths are wonderful old-fashioned flowers, native to Turkey, Syria, and Lebanon. They arrived in Holland in the seventeenth century, and by 1838, there were 2,000 cultivars on the market, including about 30 double varieties.

These showy bulbs were the soul of Victorian bedding schemes, but when the practice of bedding out lost favor, they did, too. They are becoming popular again, and dozens of cultivars are available in white, yellow, pink, red, salmon, blue, and purple.

Even the smallest, least expensive sizes of hyacinths lend themselves to informal plantings, and where adapted, they endure in the garden for several years.

In their first year, flower spikes are dense, but in subsequent years they are longer and looser. They are good cut flowers, their waxy blooms lasting up to six days. In the garden, blooms last about three weeks, beginning with the early-blooming multiflora types and ending with the double-flowered cultivars.

For best performance in the garden, plant medium-size bulbs, labeled 16 to 17 centimeters, in fall. Dig the holes 8 inches deep and space them 2 to 4 inches apart. In containers, the bulbs should be level with pot rims, with about five bulbs per 6-inch pot.

Notable for their intense fragrance, use hyacinths sparingly; more than 1 or 2 can be overwhelming. Hyacinths are a favorite for forcing in glass vases, as well as in soil.

USES: In borders, beds, containers, as houseplants
SOIL: Fast draining, organic
CARE: Water generously during period of growth and blooming; deer and rodent resistant
LIGHT: Full sun or light shade
HARDINESS: Zones 4–7

Hyacinths are often used in mass plantings of spring-flowering bulbs. Their dense flower clusters make bold strokes of color in the landscape. These blue hyacinths are growing at Keukenhof, in Lisse, Holland.

Each flower stalk of this hyacinth is composed of numerous perfect little bells.

Hyacinths don't have to stand in uniform ranks. These 'Blue Jacket' are combined with tulips, pansies, and primroses.

Hardy gloxinia flowers are ruffled around the edges. The blooms emerge from clumps of ferny foliage.

INCARVILLEA

Hardy gloxinia

- Bignonia family
- Tuberous root
- Blooms in summer

Hardy gloxinias are not related to gloxinias at all. They are members of the Bignonia family, which includes trumpet vines.

Native to India, Tibet, and China, hardy gloxinias have showy flowers, appearing in early or late summer, depending on the species. The trumpetlike blooms may be pink, magenta, or slightly purple. Sometimes they have yellow or white throats. The flowers appear in clusters of 6 to 20 flowers on stems 12 to 18 inches long. The stems may be rather relaxed, but the flowers usually rise above the plants' feathery foliage.

The roots, which look like a pale bunch of carrots (with only one top), should be planted

USES: In borders
SOIL: Organic, well drained
CARE: Do not overwater
LIGHT: Full sun
HARDINESS: Zones 5–7

8 inches deep and 1 foot apart. Excellent drainage in the planting area is critical.

In areas with hot summers, hardy gloxinias prefer light shade. Where winters are cold, mulch plants after the foliage dies back.

About 14 species are known, but only a few of these are available to gardeners.

Delavay hardy gloxinia (*Incarvillea delavayi*) produces clusters of purple, pink, or white flowers in early summer on stems as tall as 2 feet. 'Snowtop' is a long-lasting white cultivar with a yellow throat.

I. arguta can grow to 5 feet tall and produces clusters of pink flowers.

I. mairei blooms in late summer and has pink flowers with yellow throats.

A handful of spring starflower bulbs will spread to form luxurious clumps at the front of a flower bed. This is 'Rolf Fiedler'.

IPHEION UNIFLORUM

Spring starflower

- Lily family
- True bulb; deciduous
- Blooms in early to midspring

This native of Argentina and Uruguay produces 1½-inch blue or blue-tinged white flowers with bright orange stamens in early spring. Each 6- to 8-inch stem produces only one flower, but because each bulb may

USES: In borders, meadows, woodlands, containers, as houseplants
SOIL: Well drained
CARE: Drought tolerant; deer and rodent resistant
LIGHT: Full sun or light shade
HARDINESS: Zones 6–9

produce many stems, a cluster of bulbs makes a pretty display. Spring starflowers may bloom over several weeks.

Leaves appear in fall. The grassy foliage smells a bit like onions or garlic, and the flowers themselves have a spicy fragrance.

Plants grow willingly between flagstones, in chinks in walls, in sun or light shade virtually anywhere in the garden, and they will spread easily wherever the plant is hardy.

Plant bulbs in the fall, 5 inches deep and 1 to 4 inches apart, at the front edge of flower beds, in a lawn, along a walk, or in pots. Spring starflower is a pretty, easy bulb for southern gardens. In cold-winter areas, protect the plantings with mulch. Propagate bulbs by offsets in the fall.

There are about 20 species of *Ipheion*, but only one is commonly found: *Ipheion uniflorum* (sometimes listed as *Triteleia* or *Brodiaea*). Flower color is variable, ranging from white to blue. 'Rolf Fiedler' is clear blue; 'Wisley Blue' is medium sky blue.

IXIA

Corn lily

- Iris family
- Corm; deciduous
- Blooms spring or early summer

Ixia's common name, corn lily, refers to the fields of grain that it prefers in its native South African habitat. It has been cultivated for nearly 200 years, and many hybrids have been developed.

Corn lily lends color and grassy texture to a border, and it also makes a handsome container planting. Dense flower clusters are borne on wiry stems 10 to 36 inches tall, above narrow-bladed leaves. It is a durable cut flower. The stems last up to two weeks in a vase, but the flowers open wide only in bright light. Yellow and white blossoms are fragrant.

Plant corms in the fall, 5 inches deep and 3 to 4 inches apart in the garden. In pots, plant the corms 1 inch deep with five or six per 6-inch pot.

Grow corn lilies in full sun since the flowers close in even light shade. Stake plants as necessary. They prefer to dry out over the summer after the blooms have faded. In wet areas, dig and store the corms, without packing material, for the summer.

If you leave corn lily in the garden over winter, mulch it well. Corn lily is not winter hardy. It can tolerate light frost but nothing colder.

Propagate corn lily from cormlets in the fall, or from seeds in the spring.

Ixia paniculata has creamy white flowers, often with dark purple or black centers.

I. viridiflora has startling greenish blue flowers, also with dark centers.

USES: In borders, containers
SOIL: Well drained
CARE: Water after weather cools in autumn
LIGHT: Full sun
HARDINESS: Zones 8–10

Corn lily flower stems may grow to 3 feet tall. The plants spread to form impressive clumps in areas where winter temperatures do not drop below freezing.

LEUCOJUM

Snowflake

- Amaryllis family
- True bulb; deciduous
- Bloom season varies with species

This hardy garden favorite has lush foliage and small nodding white bell flowers about an inch wide, with bright green spots on petal tips. All species make good cut flowers, lasting up to a week in a vase.

Plant bulbs 5 inches deep and 4 to 6 inches apart. All look best planted in large clumps or bold drifts.

Snowflakes need only occasional fertilizer. If the bulbs cease to produce blooms after several years, it's time to divide the clumps. Snowflakes should be planted, transplanted, or divided after the foliage has withered, whether in early spring or late summer, which will depend on the species.

Giant or summer snowflake (*Leucojum aestivum*) is a mid- to late-spring-blooming native of the damp stream banks of the British Isles, central Europe, and Turkey. Its 1-foot stems bear two to eight bells. 'Gravetye Giant' has large flowers (to 1½ inches wide) on 18- to 24-inch-tall stems. It is hardy to minus 20° F and adapts readily to heavy, moist soils.

Autumn snowflake (*L. autumnale*), from southern Europe and northern Africa, prefers sandy soil, good drainage, and full sun. Its 2- to 9-inch slender stems bear one to four white flowers, lightly tinged with pink, from late summer to midfall. The grassy leaves appear after the flowers.

Spring snowflake (*L. vernum*), from central Europe, produces one or two fragrant flowers per stem, among 9-inch leaves, in late winter or early spring. This species prefers moist soil. Plants are hardy to minus 20° F and, in fact, do best with some winter frost.

USES: In borders, meadows, woodlands, containers
SOIL: Well drained to moist
CARE: Water during growth and bloom
LIGHT: Full sun or partial shade
HARDINESS: Zones 3–9

Cheerful giant snowflake flowers dangle from the tips of grassy stems. Several snowflake species are available. Some bloom in spring, some in summer, and others in the fall.

IRIS

Iris

- Iris family
- True bulb or rhizome; most are deciduous
- Blooms late winter, spring, or summer

Irises are one of the most spectacular and popular groups of bulbs. The flowers of all the irises have a distinctive three-part symmetry, but in other respects the flowers and foliage vary. There are two major groups of irises: rhizomatous irises and bulbous irises.

RHIZOMATOUS IRISES

The majority of cultivated species and hybrids grow from rhizomes. They fall into three categories: bearded, beardless, and crested. All these irises are excellent for cutting, grow in most types of soil if drainage is good, and tolerate drought.

All rhizomatous irises should be planted just at the surface of the soil. Except in the hottest climates,

IRIS BORERS

Iris borers are tiny caterpillars that appear in spring. They tunnel through the leaves toward the rhizomes, eating plant tissues as they travel. This weakens plants and leads to rot.

If you see evidence of tunnels in iris leaves, you can kill borers by pressing the leaves between thumb and finger.

If it appears that they have made it into the rhizomes, dig the rhizomes within a month after bloom (before the borers turn into moths). Cut out infested parts of the rhizomes and replant healthy sections. Throw suspicious rhizomes away and start with healthy stock. A tidy garden—free of spent foliage—with good air circulation helps protect against borers. Females may lay up to 1,000 eggs, depositing them on dead foliage.

Bearded irises are the fragrant aristocrats of the late spring garden. Planted in drifts in a perennial border, they create luminous bands of color.

plant them from midsummer to early fall in full sun with the rhizomes a good foot apart. Lay them horizontally in the planting hole, not quite buried.

Overwatering and overfertilizing are harmful. Every four or five years, dig and divide the rhizomes, cutting away old, leafless, woody portions; allow the cuts to dry for a few hours before replanting.

BEARDED IRISES: The majority of garden irises are the late-spring and early-summer-blooming (and sometimes reblooming in the fall) bearded iris hybrids. Flower colors range over the entire spectrum (indeed, the word iris means "rainbow"). They include striking bicolors and even browns and near blacks. Only true red is missing.

BEARDLESS IRISES: Spring- and early-summer-blooming beardless irises include Douglas iris (*I. douglasiana*), Japanese iris (*I. ensata*) and its hybrids, a group of hybrids called Louisiana irises, spuria irises (*I. spuria*), Siberian iris (*I. sibirica*), yellow flag

USES: In meadows, woodlands, borders, containers
SOIL: Well drained
CARE: Fertilize and water moderately; attractive to deer and rodents
LIGHT: Full sun with few exceptions
HARDINESS: Zones 3–10, depending on species

(*I. pseudoacorus*), and the group called Pacific Coast hybrids. Douglas and Pacific Coast hybrid irises thrive where summers are moderate and dry, in sun or light shade. The others are better adapted to summer watering and need rich, moist soil.

CRESTED IRIS: Dwarf crested iris (*I. cristata*), a 6-inch-tall native of the eastern woodlands of the United States, produces lavender-blue or white flowers with deep yellow crests, in late spring.

BULBOUS IRISES

Several groups of irises grow from true bulbs. The most common are reticulata iris and Dutch (or xiphion) iris.

RETICULATA IRISES: The reticulata group of dwarf beardless irises is native to Turkey, Iraq, and Iran. They are characterized by netted tunics around their bulbs.

Plants grow only 3 to 8 inches tall, but because they bloom in late winter or early spring, they are exceedingly cheerful. The blooms may be yellow, blue, lavender, white, violet-purple, or a combination of colors, and many have intricate contrasting markings. The foliage reaches maturity after flowering.

Dwarf irises are suited to sunny rock gardens and to the front edges of flower beds and perennial borders. Small clusters of 5 or 10 bulbs put a dramatic touch of color along the front walk. These irises also force easily. Plant 9 to 12 bulbs in a 4-inch pot.

In the garden, plant bulbs 5 inches deep. They are hardy in zones 3 to 7, but mulch plantings in cold areas. All reticulata irises require regular fertilizing and watering until the foliage dies back. Then they prefer dry heat. Reticulatas can be propagated by offsets or divisions in late summer or early fall. Bulbs planted in pots should be repotted every year.

Netted iris (*I. reticulata*) is the best known among the species, but you'll also find danford iris (*I. danfordiae*), which has fragrant, yellow flowers, and Syrian iris (*I. histrioides*), which is only 3 inches tall.

DUTCH IRISES: Spring-flowering Dutch irises actually are hybrids of Spanish iris (*I. xiphium*) from southern Europe and Morocco. They have yellow, gold, blue, purple, violet, bronze, white, or bicolored 4-inch flowers, borne on 15- to 25-inch stems. They thrive in sunny beds and containers and are hardy in zones 8 to 10.

Dutch irises prefer soil temperature of 60° F at planting time. Plant them 4 to 6 inches deep and 5 inches apart in fall, or 1 inch deep in containers, four or five to a 6-inch pot. Water during active growth. Reduce or stop watering after foliage withers.

Blue 'Harmony' netted iris and yellow danford iris are showy specimens in pots.

A drift of bright yellow 'Golden Harvest' Dutch iris stretches across the front of a perennial garden.

Lily

■ Lily family
■ True bulb; deciduous
■ Blooms midspring to early fall

It is difficult to imagine a summer garden without the dazzle of lilies in all their magnificence and variety. From late spring through the end of summer, lilies produce wave after showy wave of color.

Some dominate their places in the garden, others are modest in scale, and some are fragrant. One species, the Madonna lily (*L. candidum*), has even gained the status of a religious emblem.

Modern hybridization has increased the types, colors, and forms of lilies and made them even more adaptable, vigorous, disease resistant, and easy to grow.

With few exceptions, lilies are hardy usually to minus 40° F. They grow well in most of the country, although they do not like dry heat. They prefer about six hours of sun but tolerate as few as four, especially in hot climates. Plant lilies in groups in flower beds and perennial borders, and among roses or other shrubs—wherever the ground over the bulbs will be shaded. A good 2-inch mulch over the planting area helps keep the soil cool until perennials fill out in spring.

Gardeners can be forgiven for not knowing the best time to plant lilies because the bulbs arrive on the market in both spring and fall. Lilies don't really have a dormant season. Fall planting is preferred, except for Madonna lilies, which should be planted somewhat earlier in late summer to early fall.

Buy properly packed bulbs in moist peat moss in ventilated plastic bags and plant them immediately. Planting depth, in general, is 8 inches deep from bulb bases with their noses covered with at least 2 inches of soil. The Madonna lily is again an exception. Plant it just an inch or two deep.

Space large lilies at least a foot apart. In windy gardens, lilies, which tend to be top heavy, need staking. Mulch heavily in fall to protect the bulbs against alternate thawing and freezing. You can also grow lilies in large pots. Plant three or four bulbs per pot.

Ripe seeds and tiny bulbils that form along the stems of some lilies will sprout in the garden. You might want to collect seed to sow in a bed in late spring or early summer, but they normally take four to six years to bloom.

Lilies are susceptible to several viruses, particularly lily mosaic, usually transmitted by aphids. Vigorous plants resist disease, so buy healthy bulbs from a reputable supplier and plant them well. Rabbits and deer are two other major lily pests.

Most lilies are superb cut flowers, with each flower lasting up to eight days. When you cut them, leave as much stem and foliage as possible on the plant because the foliage helps bulbs produce food they need for next year's flowers. You may want to clip the pollen off the anthers to keep it from staining clothing and table linens.

If you grow lilies in a cutting garden and want long stems for bouquets, you may wish to plant some new bulbs every year.

Lilies are wonderful plants for small gardens. As they grow, they take up only vertical space. The upward-facing flowers of this 'Royal Dutch' Asiatic lily (above) rise above the purple spikes of liatris.

Tall lilies need skillful staking: something that isn't easy to see but supports plants well.

Lilies are true bulbs but do not have a tunic around their fleshy scales.

USES: In beds, borders, woodlands, meadows, containers, as houseplants, cut flowers
SOIL: Well drained, organic
CARE: Water regularly during period of growth and blooming; attractive to deer and rodents
LIGHT: Full sun or light shade
HARDINESS: Zones 3–9

TYPES OF LILIES

ASIATIC HYBRIDS: These hybrids bloom in early summer. They are 2 to 5 feet tall, with 4- to 6-inch flowers in shades of red, pink, orange, yellow, lavender, or white. Their growth is compact, making them a good choice for growing in containers. The flowers may face up, out, or down.

'Enchantment'

Plant bulbs deep (2 to 10 inches) because Asiatic hybrids form roots along the stems that are underground. Some readily available varieties are 'Connecticut King' (yellow), 'Enchantment' (orange), 'Avignon' (red), 'Vivaldi' (pink), and 'Sterling Star' (white).

MARTAGON HYBRIDS: These vigorous and beautiful hybrid lilies bloom in early summer. They are 3 to 6 feet tall and have 2- to 4-inch flowers in white, yellow, lavender, orange, brown, lilac, tangerine, or mahogany. The flowers hang down like miniature chandeliers. Like the Asiatic hybrids, they form roots along their stems underground. Species martagon and 'Album' (white) are available.

A martagon hybrid with dangling blooms

CANDIDUM HYBRIDS: These bloom in early summer. Plants grow to 3 to 4 feet and have 4- to 5-inch flowers, which typically have a heavenly fragrance. Plant these bulbs in late summer, with only 1 inch of soil over their noses.

Madonna lily

AMERICAN HYBRIDS: These hybrids of North American native lilies bloom in late spring and early summer. They are 4 to 8 feet tall with 4- to 6-inch flowers. 'Bellingham' is slightly fragrant.

'Lake Tahoe'

LONGIFLORUM HYBRIDS: The familiar fragrant white Easter lily or white trumpet lily (*L. longiflorum*) and its hybrids can be grown in the garden in zones 6 to 11 and, with protection, in zone 5. They're often forced indoors for Easter. Outdoors they grow to about 3 feet tall and bloom in midsummer.

Longiflorum lilies

TRUMPET HYBRIDS: These summer-flowering lilies grow 4 to 6 feet tall and have 6- to 10-inch flowers. This division includes the aurelian and olympic hybrids, with trumpet-shaped flowers. Others have starlike, pendant, or flat, open flowers. Some cultivars, including 'Black Dragon' and 'Golden Splendor', are fragrant.

'Golden Splendor'

ORIENTAL HYBRIDS: These fragrant hybrids bloom in late summer. They grow 2 to 8 feet high with flowers to 12 inches across. The flowers are bowl-shaped with recurving petals. They are available in white, deep reds, pinks, and bicolors. Oriental hybrids are a good choice for container plantings, but may require staking. 'Stargazer' with its heavy perfume is among the most popular.

An oriental hybrid

SPECIES LILIES: This group includes many excellent garden lily species native to North America, Europe, and Asia. Gold-banded lily (*L. auratum*) bears up to 35 fragrant flowers per stem. Turk's-cap lily (*L. martagon*) is a hardy species that may produce dozens of flowers with fully reflexed petals. Regal lily (*L. regale*), has fragrant, trumpet-shaped flowers. Other species available include *L. henryi*, *L. pumilum*, and *L. speciosum* 'Rubrum'.

Turk's-cap lily

Fuzzy blazing star flower spikes push up through clumps of fine-textured foliage about the time the first lilies bloom.

LIATRIS

Blazing star, Gayfeather

- Aster family
- Corm
- Blooms in summer

These native North American wildflowers have been welcomed into gardens in recent years. Blazing star has grassy foliage, and its unbranching leafy flower stalks rise to 4 feet tall in some varieties.

Its purple, white, or blue-and-white flower spikes look like brilliantly colored bottle brushes. Although most other plants with flower spikes (camass and gladiolus, for example) open from the bottom up, blazing star opens from the top down. It also attracts butterflies.

In most nurseries, blazing star is available as plants, but corms are also available. Plant corms in spring 5 inches deep and 2 to 4 inches apart. Liatris prefers ordinary rather than heavily amended soil. In rich soil, the plants will be lanky, and the flower stalks will need to be staked.

USES: In flower beds, meadows
SOIL: Well drained
CARE: Some cultivars may need staking; soil should not be too rich; deer and rodent resistant
LIGHT: Full sun
HARDINESS: Zones 3–9

When the flowers fade, cut the bloom stalks off close to the base of the plants. Lift, divide, and replant crowded plants in fall.

Meadow blazing star (*Liatris ligulistylis*) has crimson buds and purple flowers and grows 2 to 3 feet tall. It is native to the Great Plains, Colorado, and northern New Mexico.

Dwarf liatris (*L. microcephala*) is native to the southern Appalachians. Plants are only about a foot tall, with purple flowers.

Kansas gayfeather (*L. pycnostachya*) is native to moist prairies. It grows to about 4 feet tall and has purple flowers.

Spike gayfeather or dense blazing star (*L. spicata*) is native to the Eastern and central United States. The species grows 2 to 4 feet tall. 'Kobold' is a compact cultivar, growing to about 2 feet. 'Floristan Weiss' has creamy white flowers and grows to 3 feet tall.

Magic lilies are the hardiest of the lycoris. Their fragrant blooms appear in late summer on stems 2 feet tall.

LYCORIS

Spider lily, Magic lily

- Amaryllis family
- True bulb; deciduous
- Blooms in late summer or fall

The leafless stems of these unusually behaved plants appear suddenly in mid- to late summer, seemingly out of nowhere.

Flowers of spider lilies radiate from the top of each stem. Filaments arch outward beyond the petals—particularly in spider lily—to create an elegant, spidery effect. All lycoris are superb cut flowers.

Plant spider and magic lily bulbs 5 inches deep and about 6 inches apart, as soon as they are available. The bulbs should be about 6 inches apart. In containers, plant bulbs with the necks exposed. Wait several years to repot.

Lycoris usually do not bloom the first year they are planted and may also skip the second

USES: In borders, meadows, containers, as cut flowers
SOIL: Fast draining, sandy
CARE: Water and fertilize during growing period; deer and rodent proof
LIGHT: Full sun or part shade
HARDINESS: Variable, depending on species. Radiata: zones 7–10 (6 if protected); Squamigera: zones 5–9 (4 if protected)

year. Foliage emerges in spring (magic lily) or after bloom (spider lily), then dies back.

Plants resent being disturbed, sometimes taking several years to rebloom, so divide the bulbs only when necessary (in late spring, after foliage has died).

Spider lily (*Lycoris radiata*), from China and Japan, has red flowers on 18-inch stems. It is hardy in zones 7 to 11.

Magic lily (*L. squamigera*), from Japan, bears large, smooth-petaled, rose-pink flowers with an amethyst fringe on stems up to 2 feet tall. It is the hardiest species (zones 4 to 9) and blooms best where winters are cold and the bulbs are chilled during the winter. Some people also call these surprise lilies or naked ladies.

Grape hyacinth

- Lily family
- True bulb; deciduous
- Blooms in spring

Grape hyacinths are easy to grow and sure to please. Their dense clusters of little round flowers look like tiny bunches of blue grapes. Plants bloom for weeks. Cut flowers last in the vase up to seven days.

Originating in the Mediterranean area, grape hyacinths look at home in short grass, at the edge of woodland gardens, and in flower beds. Plants spread easily.

Plant bulbs in fall, 5 inches deep and 1 to 4 inches apart. In pots, plant them an inch deep with 10 to 12 bulbs per 6-inch pot.

Grape hyacinth (*Muscari armeniacum*) grows to 9 inches tall and has fragrant blue flowers with a delicate white fringe. Leaves appear in fall. 'Blue Spike' is a double cultivar.

Azure grape hyacinth (*M. azureum*) grows 3 to 4 inches tall, has bright blue tubular flowers, and blooms early. White and light blue forms are available.

White common grape hyacinth (*M. botryoides* 'Album') grows 4 to 6 inches tall and has dense spikes of white flowers. A form with white-rimmed navy blue flowers is available, as is, occasionally, a pale pink one. Plant bulbs 2 inches apart.

Tassel grape hyacinth (*M. comosum*) grows 8 to 10 inches tall with unusual feathery flowers. One of its forms, *M. comosum plumosum*, is commonly known as feather hyacinth.

One-leaf grape hyacinth (*M. latifolium*) grows 6 to 10 inches tall and bears dense spikes of flowers that are deep indigo below and pale blue-violet above.

Grape hyacinths bloom prolifically in midspring, and the flowers last for weeks, blooming with both the last daffodils and the first tulips.

PLANTING LITTLE BULBS

Planting larger bulbs, such as tulips, hyacinths, and daffodils, can sometimes be a daunting job. It's hard work digging 50 holes 8 inches deep. But you can plant hundreds of the smaller bulbs with nothing more than a trowel and a morning off. Most of these small bulbs—grape hyacinth, crocus, glory-of-the-snow, striped squill, windflowers, winter aconite, snowdrops, and many others—are planted only a few inches deep. Because they are so small, they fit into pockets of your garden. They also tolerate unworked soil, so you can tuck a few into the grass by the edge of the patio or close to tree trunks. Because they are inexpensive (most cost only 10 or 15 cents apiece), you can afford to experiment. Plant them with primroses, miniature daffodils, candytuft, and other small-scale spring garden flowers.

USES: In woodlands, borders, meadows, containers
SOIL: Well drained, sandy
CARE: Requires little summer watering; deer and rodent resistant
LIGHT: Full sun or light shade
HARDINESS: Zones 3–8

Grape hyacinth is fragrant and has minute white fringes on its flowers.

One-leaf hyacinth

White common grape hyacinth

'Blue Spike' feather hyacinth

Daffodils are available in infinite variety. This specimen opens to reveal a deep red, ruffled cup, surrounded by creamy petals.

NARCISSUS

Daffodil, Narcissus, Jonquil

- Amaryllis family
- True bulb; deciduous
- Blooms late winter or spring

Crocuses may hint of spring, but daffodils announce it with bright yellow trumpets brazen enough to laugh at a snowstorm. When the daffodils bloom, winter has lost its grip on the landscape.

Big yellow trumpets are the best-known form of a species of great diversity. Daffodils may be white, gold, orange, reddish, pink, or combinations. Trumpets may be flared or smooth, long or short. Petals may overlap around the trumpet like a fan, or they may twist and flare back like a jet trail. Many daffodils are fragrant. There are more than 24,000 named cultivars, and it's hard to go wrong with any of them. Daffodils are bred for success.

The ancestors of garden daffodils come from Asia and southern Europe. The greatest concentration of species is from around the Mediterranean.

Some people call them jonquils, but the term jonquil, strictly speaking, applies only to *Narcissus jonquilla* (*Narcissus* is the name for the whole genus) and a few other closely allied flowers. At any rate, all are excellent flowers in the garden or in a vase.

There are daffodils for almost all climates, and they fit into every sort of garden situation. Big trumpet daffodils are welcoming along the front walk. Showy red-cupped varieties at the end of a drive are bold enough to stop traffic. Daffodils make fine companions for perennial plants, and they thrive in rustic, partially shaded woodlands.

They also are undemanding: All they need is a well-drained site, moisture in spring, and about six hours of sun a day after they bloom. Allow foliage to ripen in the spring and they will bloom abundantly for years.

USES: In borders, woodlands, meadows, containers, for forcing, as cut flowers
SOIL: Organic, well drained
CARE: Water regularly from autumn until foliage begins to die in spring; deer and rodent proof
LIGHT: Sun or light shade
HARDINESS: Zones 3–9

Daffodil bulbs are sized by their "noses" or tips. Bulbs classified as DN I are double-nose 1 inch bulbs. These have one large bulb and two or more "daughter" bulbs and can be relied upon to produce several flower stems their first year. DN II bulbs have only one daughter bulb and produce two or more flowers. The bulbs called "rounds" or "landscape size" (between 10 cm and 16 cm in circumference) do not have any daughter bulbs, but are still large enough to produce one large bloom the first year.

Plant the bulbs in early fall in the coldest areas and progressively later (to December) as you move down the map to warmer climates.

Daffodil bulbs of various sizes: The smallest are rounds (right). They are usually less expensive than big DN II daffodils (left), but are equally reliable.

Yellow 'Dutch Master' (above) is one of the most popular trumpet daffodils.

Large bulbs should be 8 inches deep and smaller ones 5 inches deep. Space them 2 to 6 inches apart, depending on their size. In pots, plant them close together, leaving just enough space to allow good drainage.

After planting, top-dress with a balanced fertilizer or a special bulb fertilizer. Water well. Moisture in spring assures good growth and development. Plant daffodils where their fading foliage will not be noticed, such as a spot among perennials. Allow leaves to brown completely before removing.

When clumps become so dense that they decline in vigor and produce fewer blooms, dig them up and divide them in late spring as soon as the foliage has died.

A Daffodil Sampler

Every garden—and every spring—is a little different, but some daffodils are reliable no matter where you grow them. Daffodils recognized with the Wister award, in honor of the late John Wister of Swarthmore, Pennsylvania, are especially dependable. To receive a Wister award, a daffodil must produce many long-lasting blooms. Bulbs must be disease resistant. Flowers and stems must be sturdy. Varieties must be readily available, and they must grow easily throughout the United States.

Here are the Wister winners to date:
- 'Stratosphere' (1985)
- 'Accent' (1987)
- 'Ice Follies' (1992)
- 'Sweetness' (1993)
- 'Ceylon' (1994)
- 'Salome' (1995)
- 'Peeping Tom' (1996)
- 'Rapture' (1997)

Lots of daffodils are adapted to growing in cold climates, but Southern gardeners need to be choosy about cultivars. Daffodils recommended for the South include 'Ice Follies,' 'February Gold', 'Thalia', 'Carlton', 'Saint Keverne', and any of the jonquilla or tazetta types.

Old-Fashioned Daffodils

The golden age of daffodils was between 1860 and 1930, when more than 7,000 daffodil cultivars were introduced.

Bright yellow 'Emperor' (introduced in 1865) was popular in Victorian gardens. 'King Alfred' came along in 1899. 'Thalia', the white daffodil in the photo above, (1916), 'February Gold' (1923), and 'Carlton' (1927) have charmed generations of gardeners. 'Mrs. R.O.

Backhouse' (1923) was the first pink-cupped daffodil.

Unusual daffodils cost our great-grandmothers considerable butter-and-egg money. 'Mary Copeland' (1914), a cream-and-orange double daffodil, sold for $22.50 per bulb in 1931. It now costs about $1. Other old daffodils are hard to find, but suppliers are seeking out special antique varieties and bringing them back onto the retail market.

Historic daffodil cultivars are well-loved, durable plants. Many survive without any attention from gardeners. Bright beds of daffodils blooming around abandoned houses in the countryside are the traces of gardeners long gone. These old daffodil cultivars are also loved for their fragrance. Modern varieties may sometimes be taller, straighter, and longer-lasting, but few new daffodils can rival the fragrance of the old-fashioned daffs.

OFFICIAL CLASSIFICATIONS OF DAFFODILS

The following 12 divisions of daffodils are recognized by the American Daffodil Society:

■ DIVISION 1: Trumpet daffodils. The classic daffodil. One flower per stem with a trumpet (also called cup or corona) as long as or longer than the petals (also called perianth segments).

■ DIVISION 2: Large-cupped daffodils. The cup is at least one-third as long but less than the full length of the petals.

■ DIVISION 3: Small-cupped daffodils. The cup is a shallow trumpet, not more than one-third the length of the petals.

■ DIVISION 4: Double daffodils. Double daffodils look a bit like roses or camellias with extra petals in the trumpet, the perianth, or both. More than one flower per stem.

■ DIVISION 5: Triandrus daffodils. Usually two or more flowers on each stem, with reflexed petals, and a fruity fragrance. The flowers hang down slightly.

■ DIVISION 6: Cyclamineus daffodils. Usually one flower per stem, with a short neck, and highly reflexed petals.

■ DIVISION 7: Jonquilla daffodils. Two to six flowers per stem, typically sweetly fragrant.

■ DIVISION 8: Tazetta daffodils. Paperwhite narcissus belong to this group. Up to 20 flowers per stem; a strong fragrance.

■ DIVISION 9: Poeticus daffodils. Snow-white petals around a very short cup with a green or yellow center and a red rim. They have one spicy-scented flower per stem.

■ DIVISION 10: Species and wild forms and wild hybrids. All species daffodils, regardless of form, fall in this group.

■ DIVISION 11: Split corona daffodils. Split irregularly for at least one-third their length.

■ DIVISION 12: Miscellaneous daffodils. This category includes any daffodils that do not fit into other divisions.

Trumpet daffodil 'Hero'

Large-cupped daffodil 'Accent'

Small-cupped daffodil 'Birma'

Double daffodil 'Cheerfulness'

Triandrus daffodil 'Thalia'

Cyclamineus daffodil 'Jumblie'

Jonquilla daffodil 'Baby Moon'

Tazetta daffodil 'Geranium'

Poeticus daffodil

Species daffodil N. bulbocodium

Split-corona daffodil 'Cum Laude'

NECTAROSCORDUM

Nectaroscordum

- Amaryllis family
- True bulb
- Blooms in late spring

Nectaroscordum is so closely related to ornamental onions that it is sometimes found

USES: In flower beds, borders
SOIL: Well drained
CARE: Flowers may need staking; deer and rodent resistant
LIGHT: Full sun
HARDINESS: Zones 5–8

listed with them in bulb catalogs. They bloom in late spring or early summer, with unusual clusters of 20 or more pale white or greenish bell-shaped flowers, flushed with reddish purple. The flower stalks stand 2 to 3 feet tall, and their lazy stems may need staking. The grassy foliage tends to sprawl in the garden, but it does not persist long into summer. Nectaroscordums are fine plants for the back of a border, where their foliage will not overwhelm summer flowers. Mulch heavily in fall, and they may spread freely.

The commonly available species, *N. siculum*, grows wild in southern France, Sicily, Italy, and Sardinia. *N. Bulgaricum* is quite similar and the two are often confused. Plant bulbs 5 inches deep and a foot apart in fall.

Nectaroscordum bears loose clusters of pale bell-shaped flowers with purple stripes. Its stems may need staking.

NERINE

Guernsey lily

- Amaryllis family
- True bulb; deciduous
- Blooms in fall

These South African natives are popular florists' flowers, but the bulbs have recently

USES: In containers, beds, as cut flowers
SOIL: Fast draining, sandy
CARE: Water and fertilize lightly through winter and spring; deer and rodent proof
LIGHT: Full sun or light shade
HARDINESS: Zones 8–11

become available to gardeners, too. Clusters of 10 or more frilly flowers are held at the top of stems up to about two feet tall.

Plant nerine bulbs in spring. You can plant them in the garden or in containers. Use two or three bulbs in a large pot, with the tops of the bulbs above soil level.

Water lightly after planting, then wait for the flower stalk to appear. Leave bulbs in pots or garden beds until they are crowded.

Nerine bowdenii has pale pink to rose–pink flowers. It is the hardiest species and can be grown in zone 8 with winter protection.

Guernsey lily (*N. sarniensis*) has flowers of crimson overlaid by iridescent gold and prominent bright red stamens.

A cluster of nerines in the garden is a bouquet all by itself. This is N. bowdenii, the hardiest species.

ORNITHOGALUM

Star-of-Bethlehem

- Lily family
- True bulb; deciduous
- Blooms in spring or summer

Ornithogalums, with clusters of starlike white flowers, make a vivid display when planted in

USES: In borders, containers
SOIL: Well drained
CARE: Water regularly during growth and bloom; deer and rodent resistant
LIGHT: Full sun
HARDINESS: Zones 4–10, depending on the species

clumps or drifts. The species are natives of the Mediterranean area and South Africa. They have similar—and very undemanding—needs.

Plant bulbs in spring or fall. Set them 5 inches deep and 2 to 5 inches apart, or 1 inch deep in pots, five or six bulbs to a 6-inch pot. Propagate bulbs in fall from offsets.

Drooping star-of-Bethlehem (*O. nutans*) grows 1 to 2 feet tall and has nodding, greenish-white, 1- to 2-inch flowers. It naturalizes in woodlands and is hardy in zones 5 to 10. Arabian star flower (*O. arabicum*) grows 2 to 3 feet tall. It bears fragrant 1-inch white flowers with shiny black centers and is hardy in zones 8 to 10. Star-of-Bethlehem (*O. umbellatum*) can become invasive. It bears 1-inch white flowers on 1-foot stems. It is hardy in zones 4 to 9.

Ornithogalums are vigorous and cheerful. This is drooping star-of-Bethlehem, a bulb native to southern Europe.

Oxalis produces mounds of long-lasting flowers. Plants also are pretty in pots.

OXALIS

Wood sorrel

- Oxalis family
- Tuber, rhizome, or true bulb
- Blooms in various seasons

Irish shamrock is the best known of this large group of cloverlike plants from various parts of the world. They form mounds of lush, sometimes variegated leaves and bloom with great vigor.

Their showy, horn-shaped, silky flowers may be white, pink, red, or yellow.

The species described here make excellent houseplants and ornamental plants for the garden. Where summers are hot, they prefer a partly shaded spot in the garden. Many of the prettiest species are invasive.

Plant oxalis in fall or spring, about 1 inch deep and 3 to 6 inches apart. In containers, use 8 to 16 bulbs per 6-inch pot, depending on the species. Repot and divide oxalis when containers become crowded. Propagate them from offsets or seeds.

Some oxalis go dormant in winter. Dry, then store them at 35° to 45° F in moist peat. Water lightly in late winter to stimulate growth.

USES: In containers, woodlands, flower beds, as houseplants
SOIL: Well drained
CARE: Water and fertilize during growth and bloom; deer and rodent resistant
LIGHT: Full sun to partial shade
HARDINESS: Zones 7–10

Sauer klee (*O. adenophylla*), from the high elevations of Chile and Argentina, grows to 6 inches tall and bears 1-inch lilac-pink flowers with purple eyes in late spring and early summer. Leaves are delicate green. Plants are hardy to minus 20° F.

Good luck plant (*O. tetraphylla*) is a lucky four-leaf clover, from Mexico. It has pink flowers and dramatic deep purple crosses in the center of its dark green leaves. 'Iron Cross' has dark purple banding on the leaves.

Purple oxalis (*O. purpurea*) has purple foliage and 2-inch pink flowers on 6-inch plants. It is attractive in hanging baskets.

(*O. regnellii*) from South America has large shamrock leaves and 1-inch white flowers on plants to 10 inches high. This is the species sold in pots at supermarkets and in florist shops in March, for St. Patrick's Day. It is an excellent houseplant.

Tuberoses bloom at the end of the summer. Their flowers are held on tall stems, and the sweet fragrance wafts across the garden.

POLIANTHES TUBEROSA

Tuberose

- Agave family
- Tuber; deciduous
- Blooms outdoors, summer and fall

Tuberoses are native to Mexico with a long history in North America. They were introduced to European gardeners in the sixteenth century and are said to have been grown at Williamsburg, Virginia, in the early eighteenth century.

Tuberoses produce fountains of grassy foliage and clusters of snow-white flowers on stems up to 3 feet tall in late summer. Blooms open upward along the flower stalks for several weeks. They are among the most fragrant flowers in the garden and, except for the double cultivars, are excellent as cut flowers, lasting up to two weeks in a vase.

Where winter temperatures do not drop below 30° F, tuberoses can safely be left in the garden. Otherwise, you must dig them up and

USES: In meadows, borders, containers, as cut flowers
SOIL: Moist, well drained
CARE: Water and feed generously during growth and bloom; deer and rodent resistant
LIGHT: Full sun
HARDINESS: Zones 8–11

store them over the winter. Or you can grow them in pots.

After the last frost in the spring, plant tubers in the garden about 8 inches apart. Cover them with no more than 1 inch of soil. Fertilize and water the plants through the summer. They will need staking in windy spots. Check frequently for aphids, which damage buds and stunt growth.

Where tuberoses are not hardy, dig up the tubers after frost has knocked the foliage down. Store them in a dry place in sawdust, sand, or peat moss at 70° to 75° F.

One of the oldest tuberose cultivars is 'The Pearl', which has double flowers and is especially fragrant. 'Single Mexican' is an improved cultivar with closely spaced blooms.

PUSCHKINIA SCILLOIDES

Striped squill

- Lily family
- True bulb; deciduous
- Blooms late winter or early spring

Striped squill looks similar to glory-of-the-snow and many of the scillas. Its 6-inch spikes of bluish-white, blue-striped flowers rise from among strappy 6-inch leaves.

The dense flower clusters look best naturalized in clumps and drifts along the front of perennial beds or in woodland edges. They mix well with glory-of-the-snow and other small bulbs, and they brighten up bare spots under deciduous shrubs in early spring,

USES: In meadows, borders
SOIL: Well drained, sandy
CARE: Water regularly during growth and bloom; deer and rodent resistant
LIGHT: Full sun to light shade
HARDINESS: Zones 3–7

before the shrubs leaf out. Besides the pale-blue-with-dark-stripe form, striped squill is available in white-with-blue stripes, and in pure white ('Alba').

Striped squills are native to Turkey and the Caucasus, where they grow in rocky places and mountain meadows. In nature and in the garden, they seed themselves freely to form large masses. Plants are hardy to minus 30° F.

Plant bulbs 3 inches deep and 3 inches apart in fall. Little or no fertilization is needed. Propagate them in the fall from offsets.

Striped squills generally produce only two leaves. Foliage persists into mid- to late spring or early summer. If you plant them in a lawn, make sure it is in an area where you can forgo mowing until the foliage matures. Moisture in spring and early summer is essential. The best time to dig and divide striped squills is in early summer as the foliage dies back.

Tiny striped squill flowers fill out the front of a flower bed or a woodland border. They're also excellent naturalized in lawns.

RANUNCULUS ASIATICUS

Persian buttercup

- Buttercup family
- Tuberous roots; deciduous
- Blooms in spring

Magnificent, lush, double, 3- to 5-inch flowers make Persian buttercups a favorite in the cut-flower trade as well as in the garden. The flowers, 12 to 18 inches tall, may be white, red, pink, orange, gold, or bronze. The petals are as luminous as silk. Hybrid strains are widely sold. Tecolote is among the best.

Persian buttercups will sometimes come back year after year in areas with mild winters and dry summers. Elsewhere, you can grow them if you dig and store them each year. Or treat them as annuals. The tubers are

USES: In borders, containers
SOIL: Well drained, sandy
CARE: Water regularly during growth and bloom; deer and rodent resistant
LIGHT: Full sun to partial shade
HARDINESS: Zones 8–10

inexpensive, and even a handful make a big splash in the garden. Each claw-like tuberous root produces many flowers.

Persian buttercups are related to anemones, and the two are excellent companions in the garden. Their bloom times overlap perfectly, and the bright colors are cheerful together.

Where winter temperatures do not drop below 0° F, plant the roots in the fall. Where it is colder, plant them in a sunny spot in spring.

If you find that the tuberous roots are dry and shriveled before planting, soak them in water for a few hours or place them in moist sand or vermiculite for a few days.

Plant the tuberous roots in an area that will not be watered during the summer. The points of the roots should be heading downward, 4 inches deep and 4 inches apart in the garden. In containers, set them 1 inch deep with one tuberous root per 6-inch pot.

Dormant tuberous roots are difficult to store successfully, but if you try, store them dry at 50° to 55° F.

There's a hint of poppy in the bright, silky petals of Persian buttercup flowers. Because they bloom at the same time as poppies, the two make a striking combination.

Squills are a good choice for partly shaded gardens. They need little attention from the gardener and naturalize easily.

SCILLA

Squill

- Lily family
- True bulb; deciduous
- Blooms in late winter or spring

USES: In woodlands, borders, containers
SOIL: Well drained, organic
CARE: Water regularly in fall and during growth and flowering; pest resistant
LIGHT: Partial shade or sun
HARDINESS: Best in zones 4–8

The genus *Scilla* includes a number of fine spring flowers for natural plantings, containers, and bouquets. They are charming and easy to grow and tolerate shade.

The star-shaped flowers may be white, pink, blue, or violet. Flower stalks of some squill species are quite short, only 4 inches tall. Others grow up to 18 inches tall.

Plant scilla in fall, 5 inches deep and 1 to 2 inches apart. For container culture, plant one per 6-inch pot. Squills should grow in full sun in a spot that receives no summer watering. No fertilizer is necessary in most soils.

Although native to Africa and Europe, some scillas, especially Siberian squill, are hardy even in the coldest climates.

Two-leaved squill (*Scilla bifolia*), from Europe and southwestern Asia, grows to 6 inches tall and bears blue flowers early in spring. Rose forms are also available. This is one of the oldest scillas in cultivation: It has been in gardens since the sixteenth century.

Cuban lily (*S. peruviana*) comes from Spain and Portugal. It has wide, glossy, straplike leaves and slightly pointed domes of bluish-purple flowers that bloom on 10- to 18-inch stems in late spring and early summer. This is the best squill for southern gardeners.

Siberian squill (*S. sibirica*) is exceptionally hardy to zone 3 and moderately hardy in zone 1. Deep blue flowers on 6-inch spikes bloom early in spring. 'Spring Beauty', very dark blue and taller than the species, is a choice cultivar. A white form, 'Alba', is also available.

Harlequin flower is at home where summers are dry. A clump of 20 or more bulbs makes an impressive show.

SPARAXIS

Harlequin flower

- Iris family
- Corm; deciduous
- Blooms spring or early summer

USES: In borders, containers, as cut flowers
SOIL: Well drained, sandy
CARE: Water after weather cools in autumn; attractive to deer and rodents
LIGHT: Full sun
HARDINESS: Zones 8–10

Harlequin flower is every bit as fanciful and colorful as its name suggests. Up to 2-inch-wide kaleidoscopelike patterned and colored flower clusters bloom at the top of stems that can grow up to 24 inches tall.

The plant is hardy in the garden to about 20° F, and it makes an excellent cut flower.

For the best show in the garden, plant harlequin flowers in groups of two dozen corms or more. Set them 5 inches deep and 4 inches apart.

Plant them in early fall in areas where they are hardy. Mulch corms well for winter, then remove the mulch when sprouts appear.

Taller stems may require staking. Allow the soil to dry out through the summer and into the fall.

In containers outdoors, plant five or six corms per 6-inch pot. After they bloom, place the containers in a sunny, dry spot and allow the soil to dry out. (Turn the pots on their sides to keep rain out.) Repot the corms in fresh soil in fall.

Harlequin flower can be propagated in the fall from the cormlets it produces.

Sparaxis tricolor is the most popular species. It is found in a multitude of color combinations, from white to yellow to red. All have a yellow throat. Typically, a blossom is either vermilion or salmon, marked with black or red and a yellow throat. A number of brilliant-colored hybrids are also sold under this name.

SPREKELIA FORMOSISSIMA

Aztec lily, Jacobean lily, St. James lily

- Amaryllis family
- True bulb; deciduous
- Blooms in spring and summer

The spectacular 5-inch crimson flowers of the Aztec lily resemble orchids. The foliage is dark, narrow, and straplike. This native of Mexico is related to *Hippeastrum* (commonly known as amaryllis) and is an excellent container plant in a bright window. It also thrives in hot, sunny spots outdoors where the temperature does not drop below 20° F. In the South, Aztec lilies grow and bloom with rain lilies (*Zephyranthes*).

Each bulb normally produces one flower on a 12- to 15-inch stem, but large bulbs may have two, even three flowers. In warm climates, plant bulbs in fall, barely covering them with soil, 8 to 12 inches apart. Elsewhere, plant them in spring. Let plants dry out after flowering. Dig and store bulbs in sand or peat moss at 41° to 55° F over winter.

Indoors, plant single bulbs in early fall in a 3- to 5-inch pot with the bulb neck above the soil. Water sparingly until foliage appears. Repot every four years. Propagate by division.

USES: As houseplants, in containers, borders
SOIL: Fast draining, organic
CARE: Water regularly except during dormancy; deer and rodent proof
LIGHT: Full sun
HARDINESS: Zones 8–11

When luminous red flowers of sprekelia appear, you might think you've planted an orchid.

STERNBERGIA LUTEA

Lily-of-the-field

- Amaryllis family
- True bulb; deciduous
- Blooms in fall

This native of the Mediterranean area and central Asia blooms in early fall, along with fall-blooming crocus and colchicum, all of which are excellent garden companions. Planted together in groups of about a dozen each at the front of a flower border, around the skirts of shrubs in mixed borders, or in small patches along house foundations, they create a brilliant display.

The golden-yellow, crocuslike 1½-inch flowers appear on stems 6 to 10 inches tall. The effect is luxurious because each bulb produces four or five bright flowers.

Attractive glossy leaves may appear with or after the flowers and continue to grow through the winter, after blooms have faded.

Plant bulbs as soon as they are available (usually in early September), 5 inches deep and 4 to 6 inches apart, in the sunniest, warmest part of the garden. They should bloom in just a few weeks.

Very well-drained soil is one key to success with lily-of-the-field. Little or no fertilizer is necessary in naturally fertile soil. A light application of liquid fertilizer after the flowers open is beneficial, but too much nitrogen may weaken the bulbs.

To encourage your lilies-of-the-field to grow as perennials, plant them on a sunny south-facing slope in gritty soil, perhaps with a stone just behind them. The stone will help "bake" the bulbs in summer, providing the warmth that they need.

Once planted, these bulbs should not be moved. Plants that are disturbed seldom bloom the following year.

If you must move them, lift them after the foliage has died, remove the offsets, dry the bulbs off for a day or two, then replant.

In containers, plant sternbergia bulbs 2 inches deep with five bulbs per 6-inch pot. Once potted, leave the bulbs undisturbed.

USES: In borders, containers, meadows
SOIL: Very fast draining, gritty soil
CARE: Water regularly during growth and blooming; deer and rodent proof
LIGHT: Full sun to partial shade
HARDINESS: Zones 6–9

Lily-of-the-field flowers appear only a few weeks after the bulbs are planted in fall. Each bulb produces several blooms.

Each tigridia flower lasts only one day, but the plants bloom for about two months in summer.

TIGRIDIA PAVONIA

Tiger flower, Mexican shell flower

- Iris family
- Corm; deciduous
- Blooms in summer

Tiger flower, one of the showiest bulb flowers, blooms in a brilliant range, from white, pink, red, and purple to tigerlike orange, and yellow. The center of each of these gorgeous blooms is surrounded by contrasting spots.

Three- to 6-inch flowers on 2-foot-long stems shoot up from a fan of sword-shaped leaves. Each flower lasts only a day, but the plant will bloom for many weeks. Their effect in the garden is that of an exotic gladiolus.

USES: In containers, borders, flower beds
SOIL: Fast draining, sandy
CARE: Water generously and fertilize lightly during growth and bloom; attractive to deer and rodents
LIGHT: Full sun or light shade in hot climates
HARDINESS: Zones 8–10

In spring (or earlier indoors) plant bulbs 5 inches deep and 6 inches apart in a cool spot, then water lightly. Use stakes to support the plant if necessary.

After the summer flowering period, reduce and then stop watering. In areas where tiger flower is hardy, mulch the bulbs and leave them in place. Elsewhere, dig and store bulbs in sawdust, peat moss, or sand or bring entire containers in. Store in a 35° to 41° F dry spot.

Propagate tiger flower by offsets in the fall, though seeds are available. In gardens where the temperature never drops below 30° F, tiger flower may naturalize by reseeding.

Wake-robins are among the most charming flowers for a woodland garden. These are 'Flore-plena' great white wake-robins, a double-flowering variety.

TRILLIUM

Wake-robin

- Lily family
- Rhizome; deciduous
- Blooms in spring

Trilliums are among the loveliest spring woodland flowers in North America. They form clumps of beautiful foliage that in most species last through summer. Each stem bears a pinwheel of three leaves, handsomely mottled in some species, and three showy flower petals. Wake-robins are good garden companions for other woodland plants such as epimediums, ferns, mayapples, and foam flower.

Most trillium species thrive wherever the ground freezes in winter. Where well adapted, clumps will increase slowly by spreading from deep rhizomes. They also spread by reseeding in the garden.

Rhizomes of the common species are available, but trilliums are more often sold as container plants. Take care that the plants are nursery-grown, not collected in the wild.

USES: In woodlands, shady borders
SOIL: Well drained, organic
CARE: Water regularly year-round; attractive to deer and rodents
LIGHT: Light to medium shade
HARDINESS: Zones 4–8

Plant rhizomes 2 to 4 inches deep and 4 to 8 inches apart in fall or early spring, in soil rich with humus. Container-grown trilliums are usually available in the spring and can be planted at any time. Propagate by division in the fall.

Trillium chloropetalum, native from Washington to central California, grows to about 2 feet tall and bears flowers varying in color from rich mahogany to pink or white. The leaves are mottled.

Purple trillium (*T. erectum*), from eastern North America, has maroon, purple, brownish purple, sometimes white, yellow, or green flowers. The plants grow to about 2 feet tall.

Great white wake-robin (*T. grandiflorum*), from eastern North America, has white flowers that turn rosy pink with age. It grows to about one foot tall.

Toadshade (*T. sessile*), native to the eastern United States, has maroon, brownish-purple, or greenish flowers and stands about 1 foot tall. Leaves are often mottled.

TRITONIA

Blazing star

- Iris family
- Corm; deciduous
- Blooms spring or summer

USES: In borders, containers, cut flowers
SOIL: Well drained
CARE: Water and fertilize regularly during growth and bloom; attractive to deer and rodents
LIGHT: Full sun
HARDINESS: Zones 7–10

Tritonias are South African natives with white, yellow, pink, or orange star-shaped flowers along slender stems that grow to about a foot tall. They are excellent cut flowers.

Where winters stay above 0° F, and corms can be kept dry during late summer and fall dormancy, plant blazing star in spring or fall and leave it in the ground. Plant corms 5 inches deep, 3 to 4 inches apart. In colder areas, plant blazing star after the last frost, then dig and store the corms at 35° to 41° F after blooming.

In pots, plant corms 1 inch deep in fall. Water sparingly the first month, then regularly. After bloom, allow corms to dry. Repot in fall.

T. crocata grows up to 18 inches tall and has 2-inch flowers on spikes above fans of foliage.

Tritonia flowers bloom along arching flower spikes. Plant them in full sun.

TRITELEIA

Ithuriel's spear

- Lily family
- Corm; deciduous
- Blooms in early spring

USES: In flower beds, borders, meadows, woodlands
SOIL: Well drained
CARE: Water during spring and early summer, then allow to dry out; deer and rodent resistant
LIGHT: Full sun to part shade
HARDINESS: Zones 5–9

Experts are divided over where to list *Triteleia*. You'll often find it under *Brodiaea* in garden books and catalogs. However it's classified, this little-used native of western North America deserves recognition. Showy flowers appear in clusters atop leafless stems. They thrive in dry summers but will tolerate rain if the soil drains well. Plant corms 5 inches deep and 3 to 4 inches apart in the fall.

Ithuriel's spear (*T. laxa*) has large violet-purple, blue, or white flowers in umbels atop stems up to 30 inches tall. 'Queen Fabiola,' about 1 foot tall, has deep blue flowers with light blue midribs.

T. hyacinthina bears white flowers in loose umbels on stems up to 2 feet tall. This species tolerates wet summers.

Triteleia is a native North American. It blooms prolifically in early summer.

TULBAGHIA

Society garlic

- Lily family
- Bulb; evergreen
- Blooms in summer, indoors any time

USES: In containers, borders, meadows, as houseplants,
SOIL: Well drained
CARE: Water regularly; deer and rodent resistant
LIGHT: Full sun
HARDINESS: Zones 8–11

Society garlic, a drought-tolerant native of South Africa, is a generous plant. It blooms vigorously with up to 20 flowers per stem and asks for little in return. Closely related sweet garlic is similarly showy where winters do not get colder than 20° F and thrives in containers in any climate. Plant bulbs in spring in the garden or in pots 1 to 2 inches deep, 8 to 12 inches apart. Clumps grow quickly.

Society garlic (*T. violacea*) has umbels of lilac flowers on stems up to 2 feet tall, mainly in spring and summer.

Sweet garlic (*Tulbaghia simmleri*) bears dense umbels of small, sweet-scented lilac flowers in winter or spring on stems 12 to 18 inches long above 12-inch leaves.

Clumps of society garlic produce flowers that rise a foot or more above grassy foliage.

TULIPA

Tulip

- Lily family
- True bulb; deciduous
- Blooms in spring

Tulips are among the world's best-known and most elegant flowers. They are also a great bargain: Invest a few dollars, and your garden comes alive with bright colors. There are almost 3,000 named tulip cultivars produced around the world (nearly 6,000 tulips have been registered over the years), so the possibilities are staggering. You can't go wrong—all tulips are beautiful.

Tulips had already been in cultivation in western Asia for hundreds of years when they were introduced into northern Europe in the sixteenth century. They are now grown and admired all over the world. Holland is still the world's largest producer of tulip bulbs. About 24,000 acres are devoted to their production, more than for any other bulb. The United States is the leading market, but Japan, Germany, France, and Italy also import millions of tulip bulbs every year.

Tulip foliage—sometimes with wine-colored stripes or mottling, and sometimes outlined with a creamy stripe—emerges in late winter. After some weeks, it unfurls to reveal tight green buds. The earliest tulips come into flower with the crocuses, and the show of blooms continues for about two months.

Most tulips have the familiar, graceful, egg-shaped flower, but a few, including some species tulips, have pointed petals. Others have so many petals that they look like peonies. On the warmest spring days, when they open wide, many tulips reveal a blotch of black or yellow at the center. Tulips stay closed on cold, cloudy days.

Tulip flowers come in nearly every color imaginable. They may be a single rich or intense color. Others are streaked, striped, or splashed with contrasting colors. Still others have touches of green in their petals or are so dark they appear to be almost black.

The bud of this species tulip, 'Lilac Wonder', is no bigger than your thumb, but it adds a charming note to the early spring garden.

USES: In borders, flower beds, containers, for forcing, as cut flowers
SOIL: Well drained, organic
CARE: Water regularly during growth and blooming; dry during summer dormancy; attractive to deer and rodents
LIGHT: Full sun to light shade
HARDINESS: Zones 3–8

Tulips can be grown easily wherever winters get at least as cold as 20° F, but with a little effort, they grow anywhere—even in southern climates. Plant tulips in the fall, beginning in late September where winters are cold, as late as December in mild climates. Dig the holes 6 to 8 inches deep and 3 to 6 inches apart. Deep planting discourages squirrels and voles. Fertilize with a special slow-release bulb fertilizer after planting. A 2-inch mulch layer of autumn leaves helps keep soil temperatures even.

In warm climates, buy precooled bulbs or precool them yourself by chilling them in a

Big hybrid tulips grow from large bulbs. Species tulips normally grow from much smaller bulbs, some with woolly tufts at the tips. Don't worry if the bulbs' papery brown tunics come off.

In this mixed garden of bulbs, perennials, and evergreens, tulips provide the first bright spots of color in spring. They're planted cleverly so that once the bulbs' foliage starts to fade, surrounding perennials have grown to hide the browning plants.

refrigerator vegetable drawer for 8 to 10 weeks. (Do not store apples or other ripening vegetables and tulip bulbs together. Apples release a gas, ethylene, which kills the flower buds inside the bulbs.) Species tulips perform well where winters are mild.

Tulips are superlative cut flowers, lasting six to eight days in a vase. The stems continue to grow after the flowers are cut, bending toward the light, so take this into account when arranging the flowers and positioning the finished bouquet.

A Really Big Show

The great variety of tulips on the market presents a formidable challenge when you want to orchestrate a big show of tulips so they bloom together. Planting different varieties may result in a long season of bloom, but the effect is altogether different from the jolt of color you see when 50 or 100 tulips of the same cultivar are blooming at once.

The surest way to make all your tulips bloom together is to plant only one cultivar. Whether you plant 5 bulbs or 5,000, you can count on them to produce their flowers together as if on cue. If you want to introduce a few other cultivars, you have to shop carefully. Tulips in the same division (such as Darwin hybrids or single early tulips) usually bloom together, but it is a good idea to hedge a bit by combining three or four varieties. Even if one of them blooms a little ahead of time, you should still be able to count on a good massed display from the others.

Mail-order catalogs sometimes put together collections of tulips meant to bloom together. These selections save gardeners years of testing in their own yards, but every garden is different and the process of trying your own combinations will probably produce more satisfactory results, especially in the long run. Even if you fail to achieve a perfectly orchestrated show the first year, your garden will still be spectacular.

Tulips shimmer in an informal garden. Among the varieties here are 'Daydream' and 'Pink Impression', both Darwin Hybrid tulips. They should bloom for several years and even multiply if the bulbs are planted a good 8 inches deep in well-drained soil.

TULIP
continued

Expect several years of strong performance from tulips in your own garden. The pink tulips are Darwin Hybrids, among the best perennializers.

'Red Riding Hood' is a Greigii tulip that can be relied upon to bloom for years. The mottled foliage looks pretty in the garden before the flowers open and after they fade.

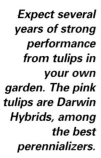

TULIPS THAT LAST

In public gardens, tulip bulbs are usually pulled up each spring as soon as they have finished blooming, and new bulbs are planted the following fall. Botanical gardens, too, replace their bulbs every year partly because the flower beds are planted at least twice and spent flowers have to be removed to make room for the next floral display.

This practice has made many gardeners skeptical of tulips' ability to rebloom, although many tulips can and do bloom for several years with little attention.

It's true that tulips bloom most reliably their first year. But if you plant tulips deep (8 inches from the base) in well-drained soil, fertilize them every fall, cut off faded flowers, and allow the foliage to mature completely, tulips are likely to bloom for at least two years and often more. If they bloom three years in a row, they're considered successful perennials.

Some tulips perennialize better than others. Darwin Hybrid tulips are the most reliable. Where conditions are just right, not only will they bloom for years, they even multiply.

Other reliably perennializing tulip cultivars include 'Parade', 'Golden Parade', 'Red Riding Hood', 'Show Winner', 'Maureen', 'Keizerskroon', *T. praestens*

Allow bulb foliage to mature if you hope to see flowers for more than one year; the foliage is essential to producing next year's flowers.

'Fusilier', 'Stresa', and 'White Emperor'. Species tulips, also, are more likely to come back for years. 'Lilac Wonder' is an excellent perennializing species tulip in the South.

Even good perennializers, however, do not last forever. A severely dry spring, a late killing frost, or changing conditions in the garden (getting shaded out before a bulb has a chance to mature, for example) will diminish bloom and the bulbs will fade away.

In warm climates, early-blooming tulips are more likely to grow as perennials than late-blooming varieties. Many more tulips are more likely to bloom again in cool climates than in warm places.

SPECIES TULIPS

Species tulips are cheerful and interesting. Most bloom early, before the big hybrid tulips. The majority are small, 6 to 11 inches tall, but the tallest can grow to 20 inches. Some have flowers like goblets; others have slim, twisting petals, or pointed petals that open wide on sunny days so the flowers look like stars. Some are fragrant.

The bulbs of species tulips are usually much smaller than hybrid tulip bulbs, and some have a tuft of woolly fuzz at the tip. Plant them all at least 5 inches to the base of the bulbs. Fertilize lightly in the fall. Where adapted, many species tulips come back year after year.

Species tulips are sometimes called botanical tulips. Hybridizers working with this group have introduced several cultivars with the characteristic charm of the species tulips but in a greater range of colors.

Some of the best species tulips include:

■ *T. bakeri* has small, lilac-pink flowers with a yellow center. Before they open, the flowers are slightly twisted, like a swirl ice-cream cone. They bloom in midspring.

■ *T. clusiana*, also known as the "lady tulip," has slim, pointed petals with broad stripes. Several charming varieties are available.

■ *T. humilis* is a vigorous early-blooming species with goblet-shaped flowers. It is an ideal companion to *Crocus vernus*.

T. acuminata *is perhaps the strangest and most striking of all species tulips, as well as one of the tallest.*

■ *T. acuminata* has red petals streaked with yellow. They look like twisted paper streamers.

■ *T. sylvestris*, the wood tulip, produces fragrant, nodding yellow flowers on 10-inch stems.

■ *T. tarda* has many star-like flowers with yellow centers. The seed pods are highly decorative.

TULIPS BY DIVISION

Here is a list of the tulip groups currently recognized by the Royal Bulb Growers' Association, Hillegom, Netherlands.

EARLY FLOWERING:
■ SINGLE EARLY TULIPS. Single Early tulips are generally 10 to 14 inches tall with large flowers.
■ DOUBLE EARLY TULIPS. Double Early tulips grow 10 to 12 inches tall and have many-petaled flowers up to 4 inches across.
■ KAUFMANNIANA TULIPS. Kaufmanniana tulips grow about 8 inches tall and have mottled foliage. They bloom very early.
■ FOSTERIANA TULIPS. Fosteriana tulips grow 8 to 18 inches tall. They have very large flowers.

MIDSEASON FLOWERING:
■ GREIGII TULIPS. Greigii tulips reach about 10 inches tall. They have mottled or striped leaves. May have flowers with pointed petals.
■ TRIUMPH TULIPS. Triumph tulips are hybrids of early- and late-flowering types. They grow 12 to 14 inches tall.

■ DARWIN HYBRID TULIPS. Darwin Hybrid tulips have 18- to 24-inch-long stems and large flowers.

LATE FLOWERING:
■ SINGLE LATE TULIPS. Single Late tulips include Darwin and Cottage tulips. They grow up to 30 inches tall.
■ LILY-FLOWERED TULIPS. Lily-flowered tulips grow to 18 inches tall. They have pointed petals turned outward at the tips.
■ FRINGED TULIPS. Fringed tulips are tall tulips, up to 26 inches. Their petals are finely fringed.
■ VIRIDIFLORA TULIPS. Viridiflora tulips may grow to be 12 to 20 inches tall. They have green markings on the flower petals.
■ REMBRANDT TULIPS. Rembrandt tulips have flowers with stripes or other marks. The color variations are caused by viruses. These tulips are found only in historical collections.
■ PARROT TULIPS. Parrot tulips have large flowers with twisted, irregularly fringed petals. They grow 16 to 18 inches tall.
■ DOUBLE LATE TULIPS. Double Late tulips have long-lasting, peony-shaped flowers with many petals. They grow about 14 inches tall.

Bugle lilies form large clumps in gardens where they are hardy. They also thrive in containers.

WATSONIA

Bugle lily

- Iris family
- Corm; deciduous or evergreen
- Blooms early spring through summer

Like most of its gladiolus cousins, bugle lily is a stately South African flower. It is an excellent cut flower and is even more graceful, in a relaxed way, than gladiolus.

Where the climate allows it to remain in the garden year-round, bugle lily grows into handsome, substantial clumps. Elsewhere, you must dig it up and store it at 35° to 41° F each winter.

Some bugle lilies are rather imposing in scale, while others are small enough to grow as houseplants, in small pots outdoors, or near the front of flower beds. Plant the corms in fall about 3 inches deep and 6 inches apart.

USES: In flower beds, containers, as cut flowers
SOIL: Well drained, sandy
CARE: Water regularly during growth and bloom; attractive to deer and rodents
LIGHT: Full sun
HARDINESS: Zones 8–11

Among the smaller species, all growing to about 18 inches tall, are *Watsonia brevifolia* (pink to rosy pink flowers), *W. coccinea* (scarlet flowers), and evergreen *W. meriana* (variable, but often having long-blooming red flowers).

W. beatricis is evergreen and grows 3 to 4 feet tall. It has pink-tipped apricot flowers. In cold climates, allow it to dry out, then dig and store it over winter.

W. pyramidata grows to about 5 feet tall. It has branched spikes of mauve-pink flowers with brownish purple anthers.

The larger forms are usually sold in mixtures or by cultivar names. 'Snow Queen' is white, 'Seashell' is soft pink, and 'Peach Glow' is apricot.

The pretty flowers of rain lilies may be white or pink. The blooms are not very large, but a handful of bulbs is enough to make a formidable show.

ZEPHYRANTHES

Zephyr lily, Rain lily, Fairy lily

- Amaryllis family
- True bulb; deciduous or evergreen
- Blooms in summer and fall

Late in the gardening season, rain lily refreshes the garden when its flowers appear suddenly after a shower.

The solitary, upright blossoms, in white or shades of pink, rose, or yellow, are held about a foot above tufts of grassy foliage.

With protection, most species are hardy to 0° F. Where they are hardy, plant bulbs in the garden in the fall in holes 2 to 3 inches deep and 3 to 4 inches apart. Elsewhere, plant them in spring. Where the bulbs are not hardy, dig them in the fall and store them in a warm (50° to 60° F) place in dry packing material.

This tropical American native may also be grown as a container plant that blooms periodically whether indoors or out. Plant 10 or 12 bulbs per 6-inch pot, 2 inches deep. Propagate the bulbs from offsets.

USES: In borders, meadows, containers, as houseplants
SOIL: Well drained, sandy
CARE: Alternate periods of watering and drying to stimulate bloom; deer and rodent proof
LIGHT: Full sun
HARDINESS: Zones 7–11

Atamasco lily (*Zephyranthes atamasco*), from the southeastern United States, has white or purple-tinged, lilylike, 4-inch flowers on 8- to 12-inch stems. The bulbs are poisonous.

La Plata lily (*Z. candida*), from South America, has crocuslike, 2-inch white flowers, sometimes brushed with rose on the outside of the petals, on 1-foot stems.

Rose-pink zephyr lily (*Z. grandiflora*), from the moist woodlands of Mexico and Guatemala, grows up to 1 foot tall and has 2½-inch bright pink flowers preceded by a maroon-red flower bud.

Cuban zephyr lily (*Z. rosea*), from the West Indies and Guatemala, has 1-inch rose-red flowers on stems up to 1 foot tall.

Z. citrina, from South America, bears 4- to 6-inch bright golden yellow flowers. It is quite similar to La Plata lily.

Calla lily

- Arum family
- Rhizome; semideciduous
- Blooms early spring to early summer

The calla lily is a serenely beautiful flower in the garden and a luxurious cut flower. Its elegantly tapered and curved white bloom emerges through a dense cluster of large, glossy, deep green leaves (sometimes with snow-white spots). In addition, the leaves are a fine garden background for the flowers. Plants may reach a height of about 3 feet.

This South African native perennializes in mild climates, especially in moist or boggy spots. Calla lilies are excellent plants for the water's edge. Although they are tender bulbs, they may survive cold winters to zone 7 if planted in a sheltered location and the rhizomes covered with a generous mulch.

Plant rhizomes 4 inches deep and 1 to 2 feet apart in the garden, or 3 inches deep in pots, one per 6-inch pot. Calla lilies prefer bright light and rich, organic soil. In Southern gardens, indirect light or morning sun is best.

White calla (*Zantedeschia aethiopica*) is the largest of the calla lilies, growing up to 4 feet tall. Small forms are the best choice for growing in pots. These include hardy 'Green Goddess', which is white with green.

Hybridizers in New Zealand have introduced other down-sized plants, ranging in color from white or white-with-purple spots to cream, yellow, gold, bronze, rose, pink, green, red, and purple. There are also bicolors. Many have white- or translucent-spotted leaves. These require good drainage and must be allowed to dry after blooming.

Elliot's calla (*Z. elliottiana*) has yellow blooms and silver-splotched deep green leaves.

USES: In borders, containers, as houseplants
SOIL: Organic, moist
CARE: Water generously and fertilize monthly during period of growth and bloom; deer and rodent resistant
LIGHT: Full sun or partial shade, especially in hot climates.
HARDINESS: Zones 8–11

CALLA LILIES IN COLOR

Pure-white calla lilies are a classic, either in the garden or in a vase. But hybridizers have introduced many new callas in recent years. New cultivars with yellow, rose, and deep pink flowers are to be found in catalogs and in garden shops in early spring. They are striking cut flowers and have a surprising beauty in the garden.

These calla lilies are an excellent choice for containers or for the front of a flower border because plants range from 8 to 24 inches tall. Most have white- or silver-spotted foliage. In mild-winter areas, they are evergreen.

'Cameo' has peach flowers with dark throats. 'Carmine Red' looks like a dark red goblet. 'Black Eye Beauty' is creamy yellow with a touch of chartreuse and a black blotch at the throat. 'Flame' has yellow flowers with red spots. 'Lavender Gem' has remarkable lavender flowers. 'Harvest Moon' has yellow flowers with a red throat. The species pink calla (*Z. rehmannii*) has rather small pink flowers.

Even in bud, calla lilies are powerful flowers. They unfurl over the course of a day.

Handsome dark green foliage sets off calla lilies in the garden.

Calla lilies lend elegance to bouquets. Here creamy calla blooms are combined with white peonies and pink roses.

UP-AND-COMING BULBS

Siam tulips are not tulips at all—they're members of the ginger family. White-, pink-, and rose-colored forms are available. They bloom from June through the first frost.

Siam tulip

Despite its name, siam tulip (*Curcuma alismatifolia*) is actually a striking ginger from Thailand. Its flowers, which may be white, pink, or rose and have pointed petals, look like tulips, but they bloom at the wrong season. The plant's narrow, stiff leaves also resemble tulip foliage.

Siam tulips start to bloom when the days get hot and continue blooming all summer. Flower stems are about 2 feet long.

Plants grow from rhizomes and tuberous egg-shaped root ends. They are hardy to zone 8 but can be grown outdoors or in pots where summers are hot. Plant them in full sun or part shade. In cold areas, dig the rhizomes in fall and store them in a frost-free spot.

Juno irises have glossy leaves that unfold like a stalk of corn to reveal many buds. Fragrant, two-toned flowers appear in midspring and last a week or more.

Juno iris

A midspring-blooming bulbous iris, juno iris (*Iris bucharica*) is native to the mountains of central Asia. The plant's glossy leaves unfold like a fan, and the flower stem that emerges from the center produces six or eight showy, fragrant, two-toned, yellow-and-white blooms that last for a week in the garden.

This iris needs bright sun and excellent drainage to grow well. Although it may reach to 18 inches tall, a 10-inch height is more typical.

Juno iris is best suited for planting at the front of a flower border or in pots. Plant the bulbs 4 inches deep in well-drained organic soil. Juno irises are hardy in zones 5 to 8.

Garden shops sell sweet potato vines as small plants in spring. They respond immediately to warm temperatures and grow quickly. They're grown for their striking foliage, not for their flowers.

Sweet potato vine

Many young gardeners get their start in gardening growing sweet potato vines rooted in jars on the kitchen counter. Now, in recent years, purely ornamental sweet potatoes (*Ipomoea batatas*) have come on the market.

These vigorous vines are popular planted with annual flowers in containers. They are even used as ground covers. The tuberous roots are native to tropical America and are grown for their striking, deeply lobed foliage, not for their flowers.

The first ornamental sweet potato on the market was the cultivar 'Blackie', which has purple foliage. Recent introductions are the chartreuse-leaved 'Margarite' and 'Tricolor'. These vines may clamber 15 feet in the course of a summer. Plant just one per pot.

Chinese ground orchid

Chinese ground orchid (*Bletilla striata*) is a temperate-climate orchid that grows in the ground. Ground orchids are native to China, where they live at the edges of wooded areas. They are happy in comparable situations in North American gardens.

The plants are only about a foot tall, with pleated leaves. The 2-inch flowers, which may be pink or white, appear in clusters of five or six in late spring and last for weeks. Ground orchids grow from tubers. They are hardy in zones 5 to 9, but need the winter protection of autumn-leaf mulch in zone 5. Tubers are available in the spring.

The flowers of ground orchids sometimes last for a month. Grow them in partial shade in loamy soil; in cold climates, protect them with a good layer of mulch in winter.

Hardy cyclamen

Several cyclamen species are hardy enough to grow outdoors year-round. These plants are best suited to shade, and must be planted in very well-drained but moist soil under shrubs, around trees, or in other light shade.

Plant tubers ½ inch deep and 6 to 8 inches apart. Among the hardiest: *Cyclamen coum*, which bears white to pink or crimson flowers in winter in the South to spring farther north, and *C. hederifolium*, which has pink or white flowers with dark eyes in late summer and fall and heart-shaped, mottled leaves. Both species are hardy to zone 7, but will survive winters to minus 20° F if covered by snow.

Like florist's cyclamen, hardy cyclamen has butterflylike blossoms rising above heart-shaped leaves.

Abyssinian gladiolus

Acidanthera is the former Latin name for *Gladiolus callianthus*, which also goes by the common names of sword lily, peacock orchid, and Abyssinian gladiolus. You may still find it sold by that name. Whatever name you call it, abyssinian gladiolus is a fine flower for summer gardens everywhere.

Plants are hardy year-round in zones 7 to 10. Their sword-shaped leaves look like gladiolus foliage and grow to about 3 feet tall.

The fragrant white flowers have a mahogany blush at their throat. They open on summer evenings, looking more like orchids than gladiolas. Each stem produces 10 to 12 fragrant flowers.

Abyssinian gladiolus grows best in sunny flower borders. Plant the corms about 5 inches deep in spring after soil warms.

Graceful abyssinian gladiolus 'Murielae' plants produce flowers abundantly in late summer and early fall. The fragrant flowers open in the evening.

BULB SOURCES

B & D Lilies
P.O. Box 2007
Port Townsend, WA 98368
360-385-1738
www.bdlilies.com

Breck's Bulbs
6523 North Galena Road
Peoria, IL 61632
800-722-9069

Brent & Becky's Bulbs
7463 Heath Trail
Gloucester, VA 23061
804-693-3966
fax: 804-693-9436
www.brentandbeckysbulbs.com

Colorblends by Schipper & Co. USA
P.O. Box 7584
Greenwich, CT 06836-7584
888-847-8637
www.colorblends.com
Wholesale supplier of "colorblends:"
tulips that bloom simultaneously.

Cooley's Iris Gardens
P.O. Box 126-AA
11553 Silverton Road NE
503-873-5463
www.cooleysgardens.com

Daffodil Mart
30 Irene St.
Torrington, CT 06790
800-255-2852
fax: 800-420-2852

Dutch Gardens, Inc.
P.O. Box 200
Adelphia, NJ 07710-0200
800-818-3861
$20 minimum order

French's Bulb Importer
P.O. Box 565
Pittsfield, VT 05762-0565
802-746-8148

Heronswood Nursery
7530 NE 288th St.
Kingston, WA 98346
360-297-4172
www.heronswood.com
Dahlias, lilies, cardiocrinum

Jackson & Perkins
P.O. Box 1028
Medford, OR 97501
800-292-4769
www.jacksonandperkins.com

McClure & Zimmerman
Box 368
Friesland, WI 53935
920-326-4220
fax: 800-692-5864
www.mzbulb.com
e-mail: info@mzbulb.com

Messelaar Bulb Co.
P.O. Box 269
Ipswich, MA 01938
978-356-3737

Grant Mitsch Novelty Daffodils
P.O. Box 218
Hubbard, OR 97032
503-651-2742
www.web-ster.com/havensr/mitsch/
e-mail: havensr@web-ster.com
Catalogs $3; deductible on catalog
order.

Old House Gardens—
Heirloom Bulbs
536 Third St.
Ann Arbor, MI 48103-4957
734-995-1486
Fax: 734-995-1687
www.oldhousegardens.com
e-mail: OHGBulbs@aol.com
Bulbs from the 1200's to 1940's.
Catalog: $2.

Oregon Bulb & Perennial Farms Inc.
39391 S.E. Lusted Road
Sandy, OR 97055
503-663-3133
www.oregonbulb.com

Park Seed Co.
Greenwood, SC 29647
800-845-3369
www.parkseed.com
e-mail: info@parkseed.com
Ask for their bulb catalog.

Plant Delights Nursery
9241 Sauls Road
Raleigh, NC 27603
919-772-4794

John Scheepers, Inc.
23 Tulip Drive.
Bantam, CT 06750
860-567-0838
fax: 860-567-5323
www.johnscheepers.com
e-mail: catalog@johnscheepers.com

Schreiners's Iris Garden
3625 Quinaby Road, NE
Salem, OR 97303
800-525-2367
www.oregonlink.com/iris

Stokes Tropicals
P.O. Box 9868
New Iberia, LA 70562-9868
800-624-9706
www.stokestropicals.com
Tropical bulbs, including cold-hardy
gingers, hedychium, hymenocallis,
and others.

Van Bourgondien Bros.
P.O. Box 1000
Babylon, NY 11702
516-669-3500
www.dutchbulbs.com

Van Englen, Inc.
23 Tulip Drive
Bantam, CT 06750
860-567-8734
fax: 860-567-5323
www.vanengelen.com

INDEX

Numbers in italics denote photographs or illustrations only. Boldface numbers refer to entries in the "Directory of Bulbs."

THE USDA PLANT HARDINESS ZONE MAP OF NORTH AMERICA

Plants are classified according to the amount of cold weather they can handle. For example, a plant listed as hardy to zone 6 will survive a winter in which the temperature drops to minus 10° F.

Warm weather also influences whether a plant will survive in your region. Although this map does not address heat hardiness, in general, if a range of hardiness zones are listed for a plant, the plant will survive winter in the coldest zone as well as tolerate the heat of the warmest zone.

To use this map, find the location of your community, then match the color band marking that area to the zone key at left.

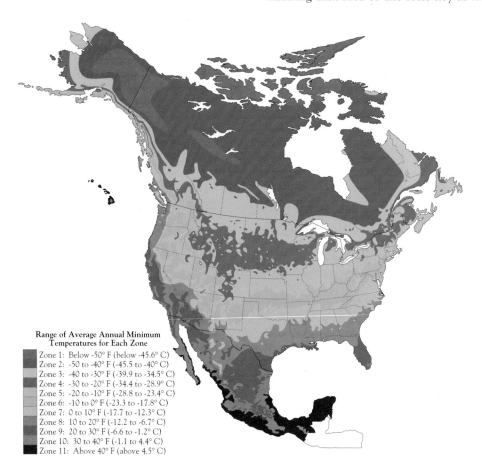

Range of Average Annual Minimum Temperatures for Each Zone

Zone 1: Below -50° F (below -45.6° C)
Zone 2: -50 to -40° F (-45.5 to -40° C)
Zone 3: -40 to -30° F (-39.9 to -34.5° C)
Zone 4: -30 to -20° F (-34.4 to -28.9° C)
Zone 5: -20 to -10° F (-28.8 to -23.4° C)
Zone 6: -10 to 0° F (-23.3 to -17.8° C)
Zone 7: 0 to 10° F (-17.7 to -12.3° C)
Zone 8: 10 to 20° F (-12.2 to -6.7° C)
Zone 9: 20 to 30° F (-6.6 to -1.2° C)
Zone 10: 30 to 40° F (-1.1 to 4.4° C)
Zone 11: Above 40° F (above 4.5° C)

METRIC CONVERSIONS

U.S. Units to Metric Equivalents			Metric Units to U.S. Equivalents		
To Convert From	Multiply By	To Get	To Convert From	Multiply By	To Get
Inches	25.4	Millimeters	Millimeters	0.0394	Inches
Inches	2.54	Centimeters	Centimeters	0.3937	Inches
Feet	30.48	Centimeters	Centimeters	0.0328	Feet
Feet	0.3048	Meters	Meters	3.2808	Feet
Yards	0.9144	Meters	Meters	1.0936	Yards

To convert from degrees Fahrenheit (F) to degrees Celsius (C), first subtract 32, then multiply by ⁵⁄₉.

To convert from degrees Celsius to degrees Fahrenheit, multiply by ⁹⁄₅, then add 32.